Praise for
Daring to Hope

"Katie Davis Majors is a voice for this generation, calling us all to a wild faith. She walks that sweet line between life and death, hope and despair, asking for a miracle and preparing for the worst. She invites us into her story and pushes us to the edge, challenging us to dare to hope no matter what life throws at us."

—JEFFERSON BETHKE, author of *Jesus>Religion* and *It's Not What You Think*

"Every page of this book is a piece of Katie's heart. It's one thing to say we believe God is good. It's another thing to wrestle with Him in the trenches and come out assured on the other side."

—KORIE ROBERTSON, *New York Times* best-selling author and star of A&E's *Duck Dynasty*

"I've followed Katie's story for years, and just when I thought it couldn't get any more powerful, the Lord proved me wrong. As I read these words, I felt like I was in the pages with her, watching God unfold this amazing new season of her life. Her words and heart for Jesus will stay with me forever, and I'm honored to be on the sidelines cheering for all the chapters to come."

—ANGIE SMITH, speaker, blogger, and author of *Seamless*

"Once again my friend Katie has painted a beautiful picture of what it looks like to lead with love. You're going to love this book."

—BOB GOFF, *New York Times* best-selling author of *Love Does*

"These are the inspirational words of a woman so connected to the heart of her Savior, she is willing to risk anything, regardless of the outcome, to make His name known. I have grown so much from her wisdom and bold example."

—JENNIE ALLEN, founder and visionary of IF:Gathering
and author of *Nothing to Prove*

"Our culture today adores thunder and lightning: superlatives, self-expression, and flash. *Daring to Hope* describes a very different kind of power and beauty. It shows how one person's faithfulness—like a gentle, persistent rain—changes the earth, slowly turning brick-hard soil into gardens; in time, it alters the contours of the land itself. Ultimately this book reveals that the most important decisions we'll ever make are the small, often unnoticed choices we make each day."

—JEDD MEDEFIND, president of Christian Alliance
for Orphans

DARING *to* HOPE

DARING
to HOPE

Finding God's Goodness in the Broken and the Beautiful

New York Times best-selling author of *Kisses from Katie*

KATIE DAVIS MAJORS

Foreword by ANN VOSKAMP

MULTNOMAH

DARING TO HOPE

All Scripture quotations, unless otherwise indicated, are taken from the Holy Bible, New International Version®, NIV®. Copyright © 1973, 1978, 1984 by Biblica Inc.® Used by permission. All rights reserved worldwide. Scripture quotations marked (NIV 2011) are taken from the Holy Bible, New International Version®, NIV®. Copyright © 1973, 1978, 1984, 2011 by Biblica Inc.® Used by permission. All rights reserved worldwide.

Italics in Scripture quotations reflect the author's added emphasis.

Details in some anecdotes and stories have been changed to protect the identities of the persons involved.

Trade Paperback ISBN 978-0-7352-9060-0
Hardcover ISBN 978-0-7352-9051-8
eBook ISBN 978-0-7352-9054-9

Cover design by Kristopher K. Orr; cover photograph by Mackenzie Dalton; insert photos courtesy of Katie Davis Majors and the Amazima Ministries photo archive

Published in association with Yates & Yates, www.yates2.com.

Published in the United States by Multnomah, an imprint of the Crown Publishing Group, a division of Penguin Random House LLC, New York.

MULTNOMAH® and its mountain colophon are registered trademarks of Penguin Random House LLC.

The Library of Congress has cataloged the hardcover edition as follows:
Names: Davis Majors, Katie, author.
Title: Daring to hope: finding God's goodness in the broken and the beautiful / Katie Davis Majors.
Description: First Edition. | Colorado Springs : Multnomah, 2017. | Includes bibliographical references.
Identifiers: LCCN 2017017869| ISBN 9780735290518 (hardcover) | ISBN 9780735290549 (electronic)
Subjects: LCSH: Davis Majors, Katie—Religion. | Orphans—Services for—Uganda. | Orphans—
    Uganda—Social conditions. | Orphanages—Uganda. | Church work with orphans—Uganda.
Classification: LCC HV1347 .D383 2017 | DDC 276.761/083092 [B]—dc23
LC record available at https://lccn.loc.gov/2017017869

Printed in the United States of America
2018—First Trade Paperback Edition

10 9 8 7 6 5 4 3 2 1

SPECIAL SALES
Most Multnomah books are available at special quantity discounts when purchased in bulk by corporations, organizations, and special-interest groups. Custom imprinting or excerpting can also be done to fit special needs. For information, please e-mail specialmarketscms@penguin randomhouse.com or call 1-800-603-7051.

To our children.
These are the things I want you to know.

CONTENTS

FOREWORD BY ANN VOSKAMP

Daring to hope can explode into a liberation out of a prison you didn't even know you were in.

And sometimes?

You don't know that there's already a slow burn of hope in your bones—until you meet someone ablaze with whispers of His glory.

Like when I meet Katie on the front porch of her house on red African dirt under a scorching July sun.

In five minutes, I am sitting crisscross applesauce on Katie's couch with her littlest girl, who has dragged up a pile of books, and I am reading *Ox-Cart Man* aloud in Uganda with this little wonder nestled on my lap, her head of braids tucked under my chin. I think my heart might explode.

Katie stirs beans in a massive pot on the stove, and one of the girls pulls up a chair and mashes a steaming heap of potatoes as I read to the littlest girl. There's a map of the world on the wall over Katie's table, and this is what I want to do from the moment I meet Katie.

We could write it on a million kitchen chalkboards: You are doing something great with your life—when you are doing all the small things with His great love. You are changing the world—when you are changing one person's world. You aren't missing your best life—when you aren't missing opportunities to love like Christ.

Love is complicated and the simplest thing in the world. And that is all there is.

And when you know the embrace of His love in a thousand ways, daring to hope becomes the way you breathe.

You aren't in the presence of Katie five minutes before realizing she never stops testifying to love and hope and the richest kind of life. She's a woman who laughs loud and long, a bit like an angel, when someone says she's like a modern-day Mother Teresa.

Katie just took Jesus at His word: real life is lived on your knees—because hope is a daring seed that you plant with prayer again and again, because this is the way your life yields more joy.

A man with a flesh-eating virus limps to the door. Katie opens the door wide and grabs him a chair, and I watch her dress his wound. Katie's hope is a verb that reaches up, that reaches out, that has hands and heart. And her hope always rises.

We go out to the aching countryside, to where Amazima, the ministry she founded, feeds hundreds of kids. We sing Gospel songs till I think we might lift the roof. I lean in and push laughing kids on swings and watch how these kids in hard places touch the sky, watch how all your hopes can swing up to touch the expanse of God.

One of Katie's beautiful daughters celebrates her birthday, and Katie and I stand together in the kitchen and make up six pans of lasagna. It's like I can the feel the sky descending to meet all this brazen believing. Katie will serve twenty-two people around her table tonight. She leans over my shoulder in the kitchen and whispers, "Pray? There's a friend named Benji coming tonight, and it's really new, but maybe God is calling us to something beyond friendship and maybe you can hope with us?" Katie smiles, radiant, and because of all her unceasing prayers and defiant praise, she has swallowed down bits of the glowing sun, bits of His undeniable glory.

When Katie lights the candles that night, you can feel the lighting: Living radical isn't about where you live; it's about how you love.

How you love the beauty of Him, how you love His beautiful people.

It's about realizing: Real life, large love, doesn't happen when you arrive in a certain place. It happens when *your heart* arrives in a certain place. Wherever you are, right where you are, dirt-road Africa or side-street America.

When your heart decides to move into God, you are always given what you're really hoping for: more of God.

Daring to hope for big things isn't about having extraordinary faith; it's about being faithful in the small, ordinary things. It's about leaning into the next right thing and finding what you've always hoped for: His shoulder to lean on, His arms to carry all, His heart to be your home.

I look over at Katie smiling over the candles, Katie lit, and there it is: Radical living, radical loving, radical hoping, isn't as much about where you move but about a life of gazing into the face of Jesus—and letting Him move you where you are.

He may move you somewhere across the world. Or he may move you to believe again, to dare again, to reach out again. But if the steadying love of Christ moves you, it will move you out into the world with the bravest hope. He will move you to hope for what seem like impossible things, because His closeness is your most cherished thing.

Too often we want clarity and God wants us to come closer. Dreams are always clear when you press closer and see them through the sheer love of God. Every single page you hold in your hands is sheer transparency. Both Katie's heart and God closeness will steal the breath right out of your lungs, and you'll find yourself the freest forever prisoner of the greatest hope.

After the birthday party, Benji lights a campfire in the backyard, and Katie's thirteen daughters find sticks, and Benji helps Katie's girls roast a mountain of marshmallows. You can see it in her eyes, how Katie looks at him, at her daughters, how she's kindled with the heat of His other-worldly love.

Standing there that night under a starry Ugandan sky, Katie didn't know yet how the story you're holding would unfold. She didn't know how she'd taste heartbreak, she didn't know how the road ahead of her would curve and turn and detour, she didn't know how she'd hold such glory—and behold Him and be held through everything.

But Katie turned to me and said, "The answer to everything is relationship." And I nodded and could feel the healing warmth of it.

The answer to every question you have is always intimate relationship.

Intimate relationship with Him.

Relationship is the whole of reality. Katie lives this in the rarest, realest, and most Jesus-revolutionary way. These pages testify to an intimate love affair with Jesus that births a hope that cannot disappoint. And you can always hold on to hope when you know Jesus is holding on to you.

For three ordinary extraordinary days, my oldest daughter and I did life with Katie, and an authentic amazing grace reigned. Hard-won peace pervaded, and at the close of every meal, Katie served her family Living Bread from His Word, just like she serves on every page of this book. And all I could think was: *You hope as well as you know your Father.* Katie hopes like she's memorized the face of her Father. This is a holy witnessing, and you're holding pages that testify in your hands.

You will never be the same.

When Benji stokes the fire one more time, embers fly and hope splits the sky and even the stars give glory.

—Ann Voskamp, author of the *New York Times* bestsellers
The Broken Way and *One Thousand Gifts*

DARING
to HOPE

1

AN INVITATION
TO HOPE

MY KITCHEN IS PAINTED YELLOW. Because yellow is the color of sunshine and of joy and because yellow is my favorite.

It's never quite as clean as I want it to be in here. As I stand in the after-bedtime quiet, my eyes follow a trail of red-dirt footprints across this floor that is supposed to be white, and tears of gratitude begin to well. My mind fills with beloved memories, so many memories that are held here.

This kitchen, this is where I serve. Many days, this kitchen is where I live. The window above the sink looks out over the backyard, all the way to the garden, where the corn climbs high and children hide among sunflowers and sugarcane stalks. It looks out at the mango tree that my girls often hang from, all happy and limbs flailing as I pretend I am not worried that they will fall. I have a baker's dozen I call my own, little girls who are turning into young women more rapidly than I would like, each one knit into our family by the impossibly beautiful, impossibly hard miracle of adoption.

I stand at this window, sometimes for what feels like the majority of the day, and wash dishes and rinse vegetables for dinner and sing worship. The back door is next to the sink, and children trail in and out, their endless questions and loud laughter and muddy footprints filling our home with joy. It sounds rather magical, doesn't it? It can be.

And sometimes it isn't. Children bicker and this mama loses her temper and the bread burns in the oven and things can unravel quite quickly.

These counters, nicked and crumb covered, the sink, one side piled high with drying dishes, they could tell some stories. They've seen my joy as I gaze out the window at my laughing brood and raise my soapy hands high in praise. They've seen tears fall in defeat over seemingly helpless situations as I peel a pile of potatoes and recite psalms to calm my heart. They've heard my tongue zing words of exasperation as another child yells playfully through the house and my whispered repentance later as I beg God to make me into the mother I long to be. These yellow walls have held late-night laughter with dear friends and early-morning remorse over broken dreams. They've witnessed confessions and achievements and the prayers of so many aching hearts, including mine.

This kitchen is where I returned in defeat the night I came home without the four-year-old foster daughter I had fought for. Sweet friends gathered around my daughters and me to make supper, and their silent labors meant more than words. I remember our first Thanksgiving prepared in this kitchen, my mom pulling the stuffing out of the oven, kids dancing happy, and people—oh so many people—spilling joy to fill this small space. Here we've played too-loud music and danced as we washed piles upon piles of dishes. Here I've set foster babies on counters next to casseroles for neighbors. Here in this same kitchen, I've stood exhausted in the wee-morning hours to whisk high-calorie milk for people clinging to life, and I've cried out for Jesus to save them.

I stand here and let the memories flood my heart. In my mind's eye, I see little ones sitting on counters, watching me bake and eagerly waiting to stick their fingers into whatever it is I'm concocting. I hear the pitter-patter of little feet over the bubbling of the coffeepot and the excited voice of my littlest as she announces that the chicks have "popped" in the first light of the morning, and I feel the way God's mercy has washed over me in this place. I see hundreds of cooking lessons, little bodies crowded around a big pot, eager for their chance to measure, to pour, to stir. I see birthday cakes—*so* many birthday cakes—frosted and decorated with butterflies and flowers. I smell whole-wheat bread, warm and rising in this oven, daily, and I marvel at how He has been our daily bread.

I think of people, all the people who have filled this place over the years. Through the conversations and prayer and comfort of this kitchen, homeless mothers have found their ways to better lives, children have been healed and become whole, friends have found rest, and people I have loved have loved me right back. People have known the Lord in this place. *I have known the Lord in this place.*

I run my fingers over knife-worn counters, and time runs too fast. People are sent out from here. People heading home and people heading off to new futures. One day these girls, too, will head into their own futures. It's almost too much, this passing of time, the dying of dreams and the budding of new ones, this growing of babies into children and children into women and hearts to maturity. And I cry because I want to hold it all forever, the Lord's goodness in this place.

I have laughed here, I have wept here, I have created here, and *oh, I have prayed here.* And in this place, I have known Him more. I haven't always done it right, and some days I feel that I haven't been enough, but I know that He has. *He has.*

Directly above the oven are painted these words of Acts: "They broke bread in their homes and ate together with glad and sincere hearts. . . . And the Lord added to their number daily those who were being saved."[1] This is my deep desire. I know it like I know my own breath: time passes, and these people will go, heading off to new places and new futures, and only He will remain. I serve meals in this kitchen, but I want to serve what really counts. *I want to offer all who pass through this place the Living Bread, the only food that truly fills.*

My eyes find the trail of footprints leading to the door, and through bated breath I ask it, beg it, "Lord, if I could have just one thing, could I serve them *You?*"

Ten years ago I moved across the ocean, from Tennessee to Uganda, full of something that I thought was hope but in reality was more like naive optimism. If you had asked me then how the Lord might most deepen my relationship with Him, I would have had all kinds of answers. At the old and wise age of nineteen, I thought I knew some things. I was going to give my life away for Jesus. I was going to change lives by teaching people the Gospel of Christ and helping provide for their basic needs. God was going to use me. I was going to be the answer.

I did not know the beauty that would find me in a life poured out for Him, the joy of calling little ones "daughter" and pressing into Him to learn what that really meant, the exhilaration of true and undefiled worship in a sea of people who did not speak the same language but worshipped the same God, the thrill of witnessing a life changed due to basic and simple provision of such things as medical care and nutritional assistance.

I did not know the pain that awaited me on the other side of the ocean, on the other side of humility, where I would recognize just how little I had to offer. I did not know that a baby girl would call me "Mommy" for years and then I would have to give her up. I did not know that I would carry the responsibility of looking into a mother's face and telling her that her child was not going to live. I did not know that I would forge deep friendships with people imprisoned by addiction I could not help them fight no matter how I tried. I did not know that I would provide care, for months at a time, for people living with HIV, desperately begging God to spare their lives, only to later find myself holding their hands as they slipped into eternity with Him on the other side.

And I did not know that in the middle of much pain and grief and loss, I would experience a joy and a peace that far surpassed human understanding. Reality would shatter my optimism, but I would realize that my positivity was only a cheap substitute for true hope anyway. The Lord would take the darkness and make it my secret place, the place where I knew Him more intimately and deeply than I had ever fathomed possible. In the middle of the hurricane that surrounded me, I would experience a true Comfort so deep, so clear, that it simply could not be denied. It was Jesus. *He was near.*

In our pain, He is near.

During sleepless nights and the death of friends and the breaking of families, Christ is all that remains constant and He is the only One who is sufficient. He holds my hands. He cups my face. He is near, and He whispers of a day when the pain is gone and I can fall on my face and worship Him forever.

Over the years, my packaged faith of all the right and wrong answers has been enveloped in a personal touch from the living God. My grief was His grief and my joy was His joy. In my darkness, I knew Him and He knew me. In the midst of pain I would not have chosen, He was real and undeniable and true. When life was not what I expected, where hope was not what I thought, He carved a space in my heart for Him.

This didn't make the pain easy. Some days, prayers seemed to go unanswered and loss overwhelmed our lives. I still lay prostrate on the bathroom floor and beat my hands against the hard tile and begged the Lord that I would not have to bury yet another friend. I still cried tears that threatened to take my breath away as I realized the depth of the suffering of the people around me, grief that would never end, not until Jesus comes back.

No, He didn't make the pain easy. But He made it beautiful. He held me close and whispered secrets to me and revealed things about Himself that I had not yet known. He scooped me into His big loving arms and held me in tenderness unlike any I had ever experienced.

I did not find all the answers to my questions. In fact, I might have more questions now than I did before. But I have found deep intimacy with the One who formed me and knows my heart. He has taught me His secrets in the darkness. He has taught me true and unwavering hope in Him.

Truly, this life is a far cry from the picture-perfect one I once imagined, with a few kids and a white picket fence. Our house isn't nearly as organized as I would like, and dinner is often late. We make a ruckus in the grocery store, and we don't get through all the schoolwork I intended for this week, ever. We are late to church and sometimes we get there and one doesn't have shoes and one forgot to comb her hair. We can be a bit of a mess, but we have a God who makes up for all we lack, a God who promises beauty for our ashes and streams in the desert and grace for today.

And I feel as though He has given me this promise: These days are sacred. God is good to us here and now, working all for our good, and He is daily peeling back the scales, opening my eyes to see. It's not what I once imagined; it's better.

Our house is always full, but it never really feels too small. Over the years we have made a habit, a lifestyle really, of opening the doors wide even when we feel like we can't possibly stretch any more, of making ourselves available to those God brings into our lives and seeing His goodness as we open our arms to Him and to others.

He always brings them. People flock here, for a glass of water, for a friendly smile, for a story of redemption, for a place to belong. He has filled our lives and our home with beautiful, broken people, and He has shown Himself to be God who mends the broken and uses the cracks to reveal His glory.

The stories I tell in these pages are not my own. They are the stories of many more faithful than I who have also known these things to be true. They are stories of those God has entrusted my heart with, and I pray my feeble words could honor them. They are stories full of truths that are not unique to me but are true for anyone who has known Jesus in the darkness and known even the dark season to be a gift.

It's a daunting task, to write it all down, to beg God for words that would truly point to only Him, to invite you in to see all of it, the good and the ugly, the joy and the pain, my heart bled out here on paper. But on the other side of this daunting task, on the other side of the risk of sharing my vulnerable heart with the whole crazy world, is the chance that you might see Jesus here, in our kitchen, here in our lives. And maybe you would see Jesus in our mess and in our brokenness and you would be encouraged that there is grace and purpose in your mess and brokenness as well.

And maybe you could read these words and know a real and true and enduring hope that can be found only in Jesus. A hope that met me in the places that I didn't expect, the places that I would not have chosen to walk through. A hope that was birthed amid pain and wreckage.

And so I invite you in to join us, dear one. Not because we have any answers, but because I know the One who does. The kitchen isn't big, but we will make room. Come on in. For a glass of cold water, for a friendly smile, for a story of redemption, for a place to belong. My most daring prayer is that you would find the Lord here, in the pages of our stories and, more so, in the pages of your own. He has been my companion in the most devastating trials and greatest joys. His deepest desire is to be yours too.

2

THE GOD
WRESTLER

THE RUMPLED PAGES OF MY Bible lay open to Genesis next to piles of vegetables waiting to be turned into spaghetti sauce as I watch the girls through the kitchen window.

Jacob was left alone, and a man wrestled with him till daybreak. When the man saw that he could not overpower him, he touched the socket of Jacob's hip so that his hip was wrenched as he wrestled with the man. Then the man said, "Let me go, for it is daybreak."

But Jacob replied, "I will not let you go unless you bless me."

The man asked him, "What is your name?"

"Jacob," he answered.

Then the man said, "Your name will no longer be Jacob, but Israel, because you have struggled with God and with men and have overcome."

Jacob said, "Please tell me your name."

But he replied, "Why do you ask me my name?" Then he
blessed him there.

So Jacob called the place Peniel, saying, "It is because I saw
God face to face, and yet my life was spared."

The sun rose above him as he passed Peniel, and he was
limping because of his hip.[1]

I stand at the sink, hands wrinkled from dishwater, and watch children dance around the yard with cabbage leaves on their heads while
they plant sunflower seeds in the garden, and I marvel at their resilience.
It is November. Life is busy. Laughter and happy chatter swirl all around
me as I silently ask God tough questions—questions I never thought I
would have.

Just last month, on a day like today, sun shining and breeze blowing,
life had turned upside down. The biological mother of one of my long-
term foster daughters showed up for the first time in the three years since
she'd abandoned her child. She now declared she wanted her daughter
back.

I have always been a huge proponent of family reunification, and we
have housed all kinds of foster children and even adults over the years,
always with the goal of getting them back on their feet and into a safe
home in the community. We've seen this to be wildly successful, and it is
with true joy that we've taken in new foster children who we knew we
were to embrace as family but just for a season. We loved them wholeheartedly too. Our ministry organization, Amazima—a word meaning
"truth" in the local language Luganda—is built around a commitment
to trying to ensure that children are kept in their homes with their biological families.

But this time it was the furthest thing from what I wanted, because this time it was *my daughter*. We did not expect Jane's placement with us to be temporary. She had been abandoned in a large empty house when she was less than two years old and had lived with us ever since a neighbor found her and brought her to our home. There was no sign of any biological family members willing to care for her, so I began the paper chase to make her adoption final by law. In my heart, though, she was already a permanent member of our family. I called her mine, and I felt that the Lord had too. I combed her hair and taught her the alphabet and tucked her into bed with a kiss as her mother. I kissed her dimpled cheeks and scooped all her belly-giggling life up into my lap and reminded her to brush her teeth as her mother. She jumped on the bed and sat around the table with her sisters and lined her little shoes up with all the rest of ours as a member of our family.

And suddenly it was very clear that she was not to be.

I felt that on some level I should rejoice at Lisa's desire to reclaim Jane as her daughter, but I felt only anger and loss at this wildly unexpected and seemingly unfair turn of events. I didn't know Lisa, and although I wanted to give her the benefit of the doubt, I was deeply concerned by the many signs that she might not be prepared for the responsibilities of motherhood. Sweet Jane was utterly confused by this somewhat stranger who appeared out of nowhere to upend her life. We were the only family she had ever known, that she could remember. Outwardly, I did all I could to ensure her successful and healthy transition, but inside I wrestled. I was Jacob, the God wrestler.

I remember that time like a slide show of still-frame photographs: Jane's chipped pink fingernail polish on fingers curled tightly around her backpack as she stepped into a car with a woman she did not know yet. Her sisters pleading with me to go get her, and my faltering words as I tried to explain with grace and understanding. Me later crumpled in the grass of the backyard in tears. My loud cries to Jesus to please let this not be true, please let it all be a bad dream that I would wake up from soon to find my life normal and my children, *all* my children, swinging contentedly together from the mango tree out back.

But my cries had changed nothing. Now she lived in a different town with a different mother who would help her brush her teeth and teach her the alphabet. She took her shoes off by the door of another home while her seat at our table and her bed in her bedroom remained empty. In the month since she left, I'd sat often on that same bed, tears streaming down my face, and begged the Lord to bring me back my little girl. He'd said, *No, not this time.*

And what do you do when suddenly your four-year-old isn't yours and there is a hole in your family and a deeper one right through your heart? How do you get up day after day to face a world of brokenness and hurt and failure? You murmur the question and you hope that no one hears you: *Is God really good, does He really see me, and how does He love us in all this mess?*

For the first time that I could remember, I questioned the God I had trusted wholeheartedly since I was little. I whispered questions that I felt I shouldn't be asking: "Are You *really* good? Could You be good when this world is so full of suffering? Do You really see me? Do You truly love us?" The questions startled me, but they pounded through my head. How would I know God's goodness, here, when all I wanted was *not* to be here?

Like Jacob, I floundered, but He would not let go. In fact, His pursuit of me intensified.

~

Life as I had known it for years ceased to exist. Weekly I made the five-hour drive to the small town where Jane was now living with her mother. I desperately wanted her to know that we had not abandoned or forgotten her, and I wanted her to feel loved and supported in her transition to live with her mom. I knew that at four years old, she would be looking to me, the only person she had previously known as a parent, to reassure her that this change was good and safe and okay. I believed it was best for her to feel that security even while I was still wrestling. I wanted Lisa to know too that as much as this was not what I selfishly wanted, I would support her in being the very best mother she could be.

All the long way to Jane's new home, I looked out over bumpy dirt roads and lush green tea fields and tried to make sense of it all, tried to find the purpose in the pain, tried to believe that God was good *to me* here and now. The three of us would have lunch and I would shampoo Jane's long, thick curls and slowly rake a comb through the tangles. I tickled and cuddled and tried to get my favorite belly laugh out of a little girl whose eyes now stared vacant and confused at a woman she had called mother for years, a woman who now left her at the home of another. I prayed over her little head and shared stories of her early life with her now-mother and taught Lisa the brand of lotion that soothed Jane's rash-prone skin and the way she liked her shoes tied double knotted so she wouldn't have to stop playing to bother retying them. I forced a smile and words of excitement over the new life they were sharing together, while secretly I asked God *why*. And then I would kiss them both and drive back home to where my others missed their little sister. All that long drive I begged Him for *my* way, *my* will to be done.

I wrestled like Jacob. I shook my fists and said no to what God had given me. No, I didn't want this. I didn't want to be this person, this family. This was not what I had signed up for. *This is not okay with me, God.*

But somehow, deep down, I believed I might see Him here.

As I thought on Jacob's story, I felt that he was too audacious in his demand of God, "Bless me! I will not let you go until you bless me!"[2] But my audacity was not far from his. It is bold to watch the life around you crumble and somehow still believe that He would extend blessing. It was not a belief I found within myself but one that He continued to impress upon my heart even in my doubt. My heart, in its search for a God who was not just good but personal, demanded like Jacob, "I want to see you here! I want to see the blessing!"

And God did not let go. And the sun still rose. Slowly, hesitantly, I found the frail frame of my faith being wrenched away and replaced with a deeper understanding that marked me for life: I would see God in the wrestling.

God began to redefine in *His* language things that I had once defined in my own. I had always believed that beauty could be found in all things. Up until recently, I thought this beauty was found in a "happy ending." I unknowingly believed that God's blessing was evident only when things turned out well. And so I kept asking and waiting for the beauty to be revealed on my terms. I wanted to write the story all tied up nicely with a bow on top. The story with the happy ending that I wanted, pretty and neat and not painful or confusing.

But days and weeks and months went by, and this story wasn't ending my way.

I looked around at my Ugandan brothers and sisters, also fervent believers in Christ, and all the ways that their stories were not ending in the ways that they planned or desired either. I knew women who were faithful wives and mothers, faithful to the Word of God, who still had to pick through heaps of trash to find something to feed their children at the end of the day. I knew families who loved their children just as much as I loved mine but had to watch them die because they didn't have access to affordable medical care. I knew children left parentless due to simple, preventable, treatable disease. Everywhere I looked, suffering abounded. This realization left me with two explanations: either God is not actually who He says He is, or He is and I needed to relearn how to know Him even in hardship.

I devoured Scripture in a new way, trying to find the answers to my questions. I walked around in a daze and read the words of Romans 8:32 over and over: "He who did not spare his own Son, but gave him up for us all—how will he not also, along with him, graciously give us all things?" All things. All things we need. Could I believe this? Could I believe that God was giving everything I needed, even when it wasn't what I wanted?

I knew that I had to learn to believe this. For me, for my children, for those we were serving. We needed to believe that God, who gave His Son, was giving us all that we needed and *that* was beauty enough, even without a happy ending. Though God did not answer my prayer the way I wanted, He answered. For all my cries and all my pleas and all my questions, He had an answer. He did not say yes to my request, but He did not remain silent. *I will make this beautiful too,* He whispered. Could He? *I have already blessed you,* He spoke to my heart again. And then I prayed, over and over again, *Oh, Lord. Give me eyes to see.*

It started with Christ, the blessing I could not ignore. *He who gave His own Son,* I thought. *What else has He given? What else do I need to see?* I was still pondering this as I stood in my kitchen one day, washing dishes yet again after one of my visits to Lisa and Jane. I pulled out a sticky note with still-wrinkly hands and wrote it down: *Thank You, Lord, for the resilience of my children. Thank You for the light streaming through kitchen windows and the pile of dishes all clean. Thank You for sunflower seeds that will one day bloom beautiful.* And then, to me more than to Him, "How will He not also graciously give us all things?" Water dropped and the ink smeared. I stuck the pink Post-it on the wall.

Could I see the good things even here? Could I wrestle long enough to see my blessing even in the dark night?

On this day, from the outside, life looked good, with happy kids in the yard and stew bubbling on the stove. Some might think I had "made it" as a Christian. I was a work-at-home mom with a tribe of little people, running a growing Christian ministry that served hundreds of children and families by providing them with education, food, medical care, and biblical teaching. But despite these superficial measures of supposed success, I was only just learning a complete and utter dependence on God and had yet to learn the beautifully tender side of Him that would love me, in spite of me, relentlessly.

It wasn't outward service or success that would teach me who God really was. It wasn't the long path to Peniel that changed Jacob; it was the wrestling. I wrestled to see good, to believe the words I was trying to teach others. My cry was that of Jacob: "I will not let go until you bless me, until I see you here."

And so I began to scribble my own words, just for me. I wrote down all the blessings I saw. Sticky notes began to line the walls of the kitchen, testifying to all God had given us. I needed to see. I needed to believe it. And so I wrote, *Sticky lollipops and quick apologies. Laughter at midnight and a warm baby in the sling. A full house with every space used for loving. Sisters who help. The wind in my hair.* The kitchen filled with these small reminders to myself, written between the peeling of potatoes and the tending of hearts and the bending over the laundry pile after children were snug in bed.

And when my head pounded with the question "Where is God in this mess?" my heart started to know the inexplicable reality that He was right beside me. Some blessings were big and some were small, but there was no denying that they were everywhere. I knew His presence in a way that I had not known previously. Gratitude was healing me. Giving thanks to the One who both gives and takes away, and remains my Savior in either circumstance, refocused my heart and made me strong. I still hurt. The God wrestler, I walked with a limp. I was still just barely grasping all that He had for me, still just learning to see. In the wrestling, He began that long process of opening my eyes. *Clean laundry, rain dancing on the tin roof, friends who listen. Mangoes from our tree, whispered bedtime prayers, mercy for today.*

Gratitude brought me into communion with God. Here God completely redefined His beauty for me. This beauty came in His presence with me even before the happy ending was there, even if my vision of the happy ending never came true.

It is Christmastime. I make sheep costumes for the Christmas play next week, and carols ring through the house from stereo speakers and off-key children's voices. Just like every year, I shake my head at the foreignness of the blazing African sun beating down on my neck in the middle of December. My mind spins with thoughts of what still needs to be done, my heart longing to keep Christmas normal for the girls in the midst of grief over the loss of their sister. We are expecting more than twenty extras for Christmas dinner. We have always loved hosting big dinners, the house full and bustling with life and laughter, but today the thought of planning and cooking for that many people almost feels burdensome; every step feels weighed down. How will God train my heart to see, to receive, to celebrate, when all our family traditions are missing one tiny, bubbly family member?

We pile in the van and drive over bumps and potholes to the local market, packed full of people and smells and dirt. There we pick out the biggest turkey, and the girls playfully argue over who will get to hold the unwieldy, still-living bird on the way home. I beg them not to name him

lest we lose our Christmas dinner into pet territory along with Moses the
hedgehog and Bo the disabled cat and the slew of other animals they
have collected over the years. We spread out to barter for our other gro-
ceries, potatoes out of a burlap sack and carrots fresh out of the ground,
and I wish I could pick up some joy here in the market with my onions.
I send my friend Renee a text and ask if she will bring dessert, as my pie
crust always crumbles. It seems like every other Christmas. I desperately
want it to be.

Later, I hang stockings on the wall as my youngest, Patricia, only
two, dances on the dinner table, anticipating what is to come. The girls
beg to decorate the tree I have yet to put up. When I say that will have to
wait a little longer, they busy themselves arranging the figurines of the
little banana-fiber nativity set, squealing with delight over baby Jesus.

In these ordinary moments, I am so grateful for my girls, who have
walked the harsh road of family lost and found. I am grateful for their
love and life and laughter but also for their tangible everyday needs that
keep me getting up each morning, keep me from sinking under the covers of sadness and self-pity. These thirteen hearts still need me, still cling
to me, and this leads me to each next step. I need them to need me. Even
though I hurt, their ordinary, everyday needs give me purpose in the
pain.

I come to Jane's stocking and wonder what to do. I can't hang it. I
can't throw it away. I waffle between reaching to believe that God is good
in all things, and sitting in confused silence.

I am lost in these thoughts as the sun creeps below the horizon. The
phone rings. A young woman, Maria, has delivered her baby boy prema-
turely at the hospital just down the street, and the doctors cannot stop
her bleeding. My longtime friend Christine, a social worker on our staff,
begs from the other end of the phone for me to come. So, promising the
girls that I will get the tree up tomorrow, tucking them snugly under

covers and kissing their foreheads good night, I leave the oldest in charge of their sisters and head around the corner to the hospital.

Not again, Lord. My mind races as I make the short but bumpy trip. *Please not again.*

The hospital is dimly lit, but the pallor of Maria's face is unmistakable as she moves in and out of consciousness. I sit on the edge of her bed and cradle her newborn son to my chest to keep him warm. Paint peels off the hospital walls, women in labor groan, and time seems to stand still as I examine his perfect pink little fingers and toes. Maria moans for water. Christine holds a cup to Maria's lips and then moves in search of a doctor. I stare at the cracking cement floor and think of Bethlehem.

I can imagine the stench.

Joseph has walked and Mary ridden ninety miles in the scorching sun, the wind whipping around their faces and caking them with dust from the dirt road. More sweat pours from Mary's brow as she experiences the pains of labor for the first time. The room is packed with all the travelers' animals. Flies buzz around them in the heat, and the air is heavy with the smells of sickly sweet hay and manure.

And into this, a baby enters.

I have witnessed this kind of birth before. Woman sighs and baby falls right into the dirt and into the dark of a tiny mud hut with the light of just a thin candle, and eyes search for something, anything, sharp to cut the cord. Water is a luxury and too far away to fetch at this hour, so the women of the community wrap the baby in whatever filthy rag scraps can be found without even wiping her off first.

I picture Joseph as he searches for anything he can find in the dim light to cut the cord and then scrambles to swaddle his child, probably in rags carrying the aforementioned stench and the dirt of the journey. Trembling and exhausted, they wrap Him as best they can and, swatting flies away, lay Him in the same trough out of which these animals have been eating.

Behold, the Savior.

And in this moment, God fulfills every promise ever made. This, God's perfect time. This, His perfect plan. And His promise is simple and at the same time unbelievable: Emmanuel, *God is with us.* God Himself, right here in our mess. *Even right here in my less-than-ideal Christmas, He remains the only provision I need.*

He makes Himself very least, no more status or opportunity than the helpless infant I cradle, than the woman who bleeds out beside me on the bed. He makes Himself very least so that He can commune with the most desperate: us. And to the humblest, the shepherds, He sends His messengers, to call them to see. Only those who are desperate and poor and unassuming can behold the miracle that night.

He is here. God with us, here in the mess. Here in the home that is missing a four-year-old and here in the overcrowded, understaffed hospital, here on the rickety tin-frame bed in the light of the lantern. And the wretched condition of our hearts is worse than the wretched condition of this hospital, and the stench of our sin and our doubt much more potent than the stench of a barn, but that does not deter Him, God with us.

Am I humble enough to see?

Behold, the Savior.

My mind jolts back to reality when Maria heaves a sigh, as her very last breath escapes her lips. Her baby cries in my arms, hungry.

3

IN THE THICKET

EARLY THE NEXT MORNING, after just a few hours' rest at home, I sit in the child-welfare office to fill out temporary foster papers that will allow Maria's tiny baby, Gift, to stay with us while we search out his relatives. Paperwork in hand, I go back to the hospital to collect him. Then, newborn bundled tightly to my chest, I head for home. I look at a little boy who lost his mother just as the sun crept back over the horizon. I look at my hands, which have loved many, only to watch them go. And I make a list of blessings in my head, even without a sticky note: *Christmas carols, newborn-baby fingernails, children who will be so excited to welcome this little one.*

I look at his sweet baby face, and hope surges up in me at this new life. Instantly, grief shadows the hope as I wonder, *Where will he go? Who will he be? Will he have a family?* I am happy to have a baby in our home at Christmastime but overwhelmed with the brokenness of the world. I wrestle.

As we come home, the girls race to the van, anticipating the arrival of our tiny guest. They shriek and ooh and ahh and clamor to be the first to hold him. His curly black hair pokes up out of the top of his blanket as their little hands pull it back to peek at his face. We behold the face of God in the tiny face of a baby, and I know that we will love him. Christmas carols stream from the house, and my hope swells.

As I look down at the baby cradled in my arms, his little finger clutched around mine, I think of Abraham of the Bible, whom God instructed, "Leave your country, your people and your father's household and go to the land I will show you."[1] I'm not walking into a new land, but as I walk back into my house without the daughter I long for and carrying a baby who isn't mine, I feel a bit like Abraham. I wonder, *What are you asking me to step into, God? And why here and why now and why me?* Did Abraham have these questions?

God sent Abraham blindly, but He sent him with a promise: "I will make you into a great nation and I will bless you; I will make your name great, and you will be a blessing."[2] As Abraham traveled, the Lord showed him new places, gave him new promises: "I am your shield," God promised, "your very great reward."[3] And Abraham put his hope and trust in God. He believed Him, and it was credited to him as righteousness.[4]

I hand baby Gift to my oldest, Prossy, who wants to give him a bath, and then I go find my Bible and a cup of coffee. I flip to Genesis. I am struck that it is not being the father of nations that is Abraham's reward. It is not the vast amounts of land God promises to give his offspring or the son God gifts him in his old age. *It is God Himself, our very great reward.*

I was walking blindly into a new season, a place that didn't line up with my plans and dreams for the coming new year. A place that I never would have chosen, never wished or asked for. But God's promise to Abraham spoke to me. God wasn't promising me ease. He wasn't promising that things would go as planned. He wasn't promising a world without trouble, without heartbreak along the way. He was promising me *Himself.*

God with us. Our very great reward.

We put up the tree, and I gazed at the homemade gourd angel on top. The angel had said of Mary, "Blessed is she who has believed that the Lord would fulfill his promises to her!"[5] And this blessing isn't always what we think—the happy ending we wanted and the desires of our hearts fulfilled. Blessed is she who believes His promises. This blessing is different from blessing as the world sees it. It isn't an easy life or one of success. Blessing is that as we find ourselves in a place that God has yet to explain, may never explain, a place or a life that doesn't line up with what we had in mind, He gives us a promise like He gave to Abraham. It is the promise of Emmanuel, God with us. He will be here with us, our reward.

I have walked alongside family members and friends who have wrestled too, who have been yanked down by the weight of their tears, who have sobbed, "I didn't think it would end up this way." I have stood with friends who have cried out in desperation, "Is this always going to be how it is?" and I've watched them beg the Father, "How long, O Lord?"[6] I've stood with them, our hands held together, pleading for Him to show up. Sometimes the blessing is a hard road and an uncertain calling. I think of Abraham's faithful exodus from Ur and later his long trek up Mount Moriah. And I think of Jacob. *Sometimes the blessing is in the wrestling, because though we are wounded, we ache to see the face of God.*

Little did I know that these lessons God was teaching me in the quiet spaces of an otherwise noisy season were not just for us, not just for little baby Gift. He was preparing my heart for something that would stretch me even more than I had imagined.

A few months later on a Monday, the gate rattled open. There stood Jane and her mother. Lisa had lost her job and been evicted from their small home. They needed a place to stay while she looked for work. Jane was sicker than I had ever seen her, and their need for help and restoration was clear. So we opened the gate, and my heart, a little wider. My children excitedly accepted them into our guest room while my heart wrenched and my wounds reopened and I did my very best to put into practice all I had believed on paper. Sometimes you lead with the will and the heart follows.

I wanted to love them. I wanted to obey God. I wanted to do what was very best for this family, even if it didn't bring about the resolution I selfishly wanted. I had been learning to see His goodness, just barely believing it, and now the situation that had me reeling was no longer five hours away; it was down my hallway.

I would wrestle again. I would learn to be thankful for a season to love them, a season to strengthen their new family of two, before they moved out again. I watched Jane's mother parent, and I tried to teach without criticizing. I opened my Bible to teach her the Word, even when she was unreceptive. I watched my Jane behave in ways I'd never seen in her before and grumbled because it was different and foreign. My own daughter, whom I know better than anyone else does, was talking and gesturing and acting like her first mother, in my own living room. I had been replaced.

It wasn't the neatly wrapped-up story that I had asked for. The thing that I thought I wanted—my daughter back—well, this wasn't how I wanted it and it wasn't what I wanted anymore. I shut myself in my room at night and complained to God just as much as I wrestled.

My heart was drawn back to the story of Abraham and his faith in God's promise:

Some time later God tested Abraham. He said to him,
"Abraham!"

"Here I am," he replied.

Then God said, "Take your son, your only son, Isaac,
whom you love, and go to the region of Moriah. Sacrifice
him there as a burnt offering on one of the mountains I will
tell you about."

Early the next morning Abraham got up and saddled his
donkey.[7]

I cannot imagine the pain or confusion of Abraham as he loads his
donkey with firewood, as he treks up the pebbly mountain next to his
beloved son. This is the son whom he prayed for. This is the son that God
Himself promised to him, to make him a great nation. He had promised
an everlasting covenant to this son and his descendants, and now He
would take him away? And yet faithfully, Abraham loads the donkey
and climbs the mountain.

How I long to know this blind trust. And He was teaching me. This
is the kind of trust God wanted me to know of Him as we opened our
home, and our hearts, wider. To baby Gift, to Jane and Lisa, to pain that
would make us stronger, to the God who would fulfill His promises
without fail.

I envision Isaac plodding along next to his father, the firewood on his
back. Genesis says that Abraham carried the knife and the fire, and I
wonder if his hands trembled with the unknown, with the weight of the
task that the Lord had asked of him.

Isaac spoke up and said to his father Abraham, "Father?"

"Yes, my son?" Abraham replied.

"The fire and wood are here," Isaac said, "but where is
the lamb for the burnt offering?"

Abraham answered, "God himself will provide the lamb
for the burnt offering, my son."[8]

It is a bold claim that he makes, unwavering, before he can see any
proof of it: "God will provide the lamb." Abraham is so certain. Do I
believe this? That whatever the mountain is, no matter how steep or
seemingly hopeless, though the pebbles slip under my feet as I trudge
onward, God will provide? That no matter what I've been asked to sacrifice, God will provide? God will provide the strength, God will provide
the grace, God will provide the way?

Isn't this what I read in Romans? What I wrote on that hot-pink
sticky note? He who did not spare His own Son will also give us all we
need.

Abraham builds his altar and piles it with wood. He binds his son
there and reaches out his hand to slay him. His trust in God to provide a
way out is unimaginable. And just as he lifts his hand, he hears a voice
from heaven call his name, stopping him, instructing him to lay aside his
knife.

"Abraham looked and there in a thicket he saw a ram caught by its
horns."

I weep. There in a thicket, a ram. A way.

"So Abraham called that place The LORD Will Provide."[9]

And I know that it is true; not only did God provide a ram, but He
provided the Lamb. He didn't just spare Abraham's son; He provided
His Son. He spared us too.

And if He would indeed give His very own Son, our Lamb in the
thicket, hung on the cross as the offering in place of you and me, then
certainly all our unexpected places are also named The Lord Will Pro-

vide. In place of our certain death, He gave His own Son. I could trust Him to give me what I needed here too.

Sometimes we feel that we're carrying the knife, climbing that mountain with our faces set against the wind and wondering all the long way why God would call us to this, how He could ask this of us. But years later, I know this to be undeniably true: God, who did not spare His own Son, will provide what we need, when we need it, even when we do not know what we need or that we need it.

God sees you and me in our pain and our brokenness. He sees you walking a difficult path when the sun goes down and your life is a far cry from that which you expected or dreamed up. He sees you, dear friend, when the ending of the story is not the one that you yearned for and your prayers seem unanswered and it all just feels like a bit of a mess. He wants to name these places The Lord Will Provide. In the places where you thought life might be easier, when you thought things might be different, when you thought *you* might be better, be more, God provides His Son, who meets you and provides grace for your gaps and light in your darkness.

His deep desire is for us—that we would know His love in these unexpected broken places and that we would know the true hope found only in His Son Jesus, the Lamb, who never, ever stops reaching out for us, who cups our pain in His nail-scarred palms and cradles our hearts close to His. He wants to be our reward.

It is a bold claim, to look up your mountain, to look out over the dry, cracked places and the barren places and the broken places, outcomes yet unknown, and call the place The Lord Will Provide, to believe that He will when we cannot yet see how. But perhaps that was the offering He was looking for in the first place. Just the believing. Just the hoping. Just the trusting. Just that our hearts would say, would truly know that "God will provide the lamb, my son."[10] Because He did. And He does.

By the grace of God alone and nothing of myself, He gave me eyes to see beyond my self-pity, to see that I was not the only one hurting. What about Lisa? What did it feel like as a mother not to be able to provide for your daughter? Was it humiliating for her to show up at our gate and ask for help? Was she, too, wondering where God's goodness could be in all this, how He would be good to *her* and her daughter? *Maybe we are all God wrestlers.* He revealed to me that in this season, my call was compassion, a true compassion that hurt for not just my own loss but the hurt and loss of another. My call was to trust in Him, even in the midst of uncertainty.

And so we walked through the season of extra pairs of sandals at the door and extra hearts to tend under our roof. I learned again to give Jesus the confusion of a temporarily undefined role in my once daughter's life, and I learned to smile in gratitude at the gift of just one more day with her here in our home. I learned to look past my own pain and dive into the pain of others, believing that God had a purpose in all of it. It was not easy. It required the discipline of a one-day-at-a-time love offering back to Him. Two steps forward, one step back. Up the mountain. And He did not let go.

Meanwhile, I kept recording on sticky notes the things God gave me: *Sleepy-baby snuggles. Pink laundry flapping on the line. The encouragement of a friend. The provision of enough for today. Flip-flops piled in the entryway. Watermelon juice on eager chins. Hurt that draws us closer to Him. A home where strangers become family.* Soon sticky notes lined all the walls of the kitchen as I proclaimed to myself and anyone else who cared to know that God was my provider, even when my flesh seized on the concern of not having and not being enough. I looked around at the tacky-looking neon-colored pieces of paper that were taking over the walls, and I saw His provision that not only did not run out but in itself was extravagant, abundantly more than what we needed or deserved.

As I was writing these things down one day, bent over my Post-its at the counter, furiously scribbling the gifts so that I could remember, my friend Patrick knocked on the door. This man and his wife have been dear to me since the day I moved into their neighbor's house, where I stayed in my very first months of living in Uganda. They taught me all the quirks of the culture, to always take my shoes off when entering a home, despite the floor being made of dirt, and to eat everything on my plate to avoid offending my host, no matter how full I felt or how much I liked the food. When I started a grease fire because I had never made popcorn in a saucepan on the stove, and when I had no idea how to debone a fresh fish to cook for dinner, and when I got lost countless times because I could not communicate to my driver through the language barrier, Patrick and Celestine came to my rescue. Their six beautiful daughters had been among the first children to steal my heart with their joy and generosity. These people had been my first true friends in this country.

Now we lived farther from each other, and it was unusual for Patrick to stop by my kitchen unannounced. I beamed when I saw him, and I could tell he had something to say, something that appeared to make him nervous. I made small talk, asking about his wife and children, trying to create a safe and comfortable space for him to broach whatever topic had brought him here. The whole time I spoke, his eyes did not leave the babe sleeping soundly in Prossy's arms on the nearby couch.

"I came because . . . my wife and I . . ." Patrick paused as if he could feel the weight of the words he was about to speak. "We feel that we would love to have baby Gift in the way that you have your children. It seems that it is what God would love us to do as well."

I stood, stunned. My eyes welled with tears and I whispered, "Oh, Patrick. Adoption! We call it adoption. And I would also love baby Gift to have your family in that way."

I pictured Gift's mother's face, pale against the rickety, moonlit hospital bed.

Government officers and Amazima's social workers had searched for other family and found none. The big girls and I had stayed up nights with this sweet babe and wondered what his life would hold, what God's plan for him might possibly be. And now, a family. God's provision. A ram in the thicket.

Weeks later, after many visits to that same office I'd sat in the morning after his mother's death, Gift became an official member of Patrick and Celestine's family, their first son. A son they had longed and prayed for.

Six years have passed, and I see Gift and Patrick's family weekly. You would never know that he was adopted; in fact, sometimes even I forget. He follows his father around the farm, helping in whatever way he can, walking exactly like his dad, and I swear he has Celestine's eyes. His big sisters dote on him and carry him around and dress him in girl clothes just for fun, and he chases dogs and chickens like any other happy little brother.

Redemption is that way, isn't it? So often, we don't get to see it. We hope and we pray and God says, "Trust me for the redemption that you can't see yet. Trust me to provide." And then every once in a while, we do. We get to see a big and joyous happy ending here and now and be reminded of the happiest of endings promised to us in eternity. We walk these roads and we wonder at God's plan, but because of His promised Lamb, one day we will find ourselves face to face with our Father, adopted as sons and daughters. A family.

4

WOUNDED

"YOU ARE RIGHT, YOU KNOW," he says. I stop and look up from the clean white gauze I am stretching across his leg. Mack is a man of few words, and when he speaks, it is always worth listening.

"Right about what?" I question.

"That thing you say, about God working all things for our good. If I hadn't hurt my leg, we wouldn't be friends now. I wouldn't know you, and maybe I wouldn't know Jesus. This leg, it was bad. But now it is good, you know?"

I know. But most days, I still need reminding. God isn't just good, but He is working *all things* for *our good*. God isn't just good; He is good *to me*. I know this truth the way I know the warmth of the sun on my skin, but God has been patient with me, teaching me, whispering to me, pressing it into my heart even when it is too hard to believe. And just as the sun rises each morning, He reminds me of this truth daily, today through the words of this once stranger I now call friend.

God has been teaching me His goodness almost since I can remember, but the most intense lessons have come this year, in the wake of Jane's departure and Maria's death and in the complications of sharing our home with Lisa and Jane and in the unexpected events that brought the friendship of this man whose leg I am bandaging. It is November again. I look back down at the very small wound on his leg and recall the gaping hole that was there when we started nearly eight months ago. I hear the laughter of children ring through my yard, and I remember the gaping hole left in my heart just over a year ago when Jane was unexpectedly torn from my arms—a year in which I wrestled to find hope and recognize signs of God's goodness and beauty amid the brokenness.

Just before Mack entered our lives, Lisa and Jane had lived with us for two excruciating months—months with lots of loving and lots of encouraging, and many days when I felt that my heart was being ripped out of my chest as my baby girl learned to not only call Lisa "Mom" but relate to her as her mother. I turned to God to protest what seemed so unfair, so much to ask of me.

"I just don't think I can take any more, God. I don't have enough. I can't give enough. Not enough grace, not enough love, not enough strength, not enough time."

His whisper, resilient, *My Son, is my Son enough? He who did not spare His own Son but willingly gave Him up for us, how will He not also . . .*

"It's too much, Lord."

Child, I am much, much more.

I flipped again to 1 Kings 17, the story of the widow at Zarephath, one that I had been led to repeatedly after Jane's initial departure from our home. Over and over, this widow reminds me of who I desire to be, and the end result of provision speaks so clearly of who our God is. I hear the desperation in her rough, scratchy voice, see the bags under her eyes as she wearily replies to the prophet, "I don't have any bread—only a handful of flour in a jar and a little oil in a jug. I am gathering a few sticks to take home and make a meal for myself and my son, that we may eat it—and die."[1]

I know this kind of desperation. But the prophet knows more. And he says to her,

> Don't be afraid. Go home and do as you have said. But first make
> a small cake of bread for me from what you have and bring it to
> me, and then make something for yourself and your son. For this
> is what the LORD, the God of Israel, says: "The jar of flour will
> not be used up and the jug of oil will not run dry until the day
> the LORD gives rain on the land."[2]

First, trust. First, give all you have. So she went. And she did exactly what he said, though it made absolutely no sense, though she had absolutely nothing left to give.

Do I know this kind of trust? I wanted to.

The widow was faithful with the little she had to give, the little that she thought surely would not be enough, and God was faithful to provide more, exactly enough, exactly when needed. He was enough. The flour was not used up and the jug of oil did not run dry until the Lord sent rain on the land, just as He had said. *Be faithful with the little you have been given*, He said. *I will be faithful with the rest. You do not have enough. I will be enough.*

And He was.

Though I felt beaten and worn, every ounce of my character having been tested during this time, I learned the beautiful trust and full dependence that came with completely surrendering my will to His. The surrender was painful, and it didn't leave us unmarked. Each one of us would carry scars from this season and the loss of a sister, daughter, and friend for the second time. Months later, Amazima had found Lisa a job and we had enrolled Jane in kindergarten. Now it was time for them to move out on their own again, to be their own family—still good friends but separate from us. I knew it and at the same time didn't want it. I couldn't stand the thought of saying goodbye again, even if we would still see them routinely.

This still wasn't really the way I wanted the story to end. I was still scared that Lisa might not be able to hold on to her job, that Jane would not get the care she needed or the love for which she hungered. I worried that Lisa might not come to know God and that, as a result, Jane might forget what she had learned of His love in a few short years in our home. But my knowledge is limited and God's is not. He kept reminding me that I wasn't the writer of this story and that when I tried to write all the endings, wrapping them up in neat little packages, I was diminishing who He was and all He could do. He was asking me to trust Him, to believe that He would bring about His own glory even when I couldn't see it.

A faith that trusts Him only when the ending is good is a fickle faith. A faith that trusts Him regardless of the outcome is real. This was the faith of Abraham as he climbed Mount Moriah, fully expectant that God would provide the lamb. This was the faith of the widow, using up her remaining flour and waiting for God to provide more. This was how I desired to live: completely surrendering the way I would write the story in exchange for eyes wide open to seeing how He would write it. In surrender and trust, I would find His promised beauty for ashes.

So we packed Jane and Lisa's few belongings into our van and drove them to their small house, fifteen minutes from ours. The full weight of this reality hit me all over again as little Jane waved goodbye, my wounded heart breaking open in all the old places.

Sometime in April, about the time that Lisa and Jane moved out, my friend Christine pulled up in our ministry van. "I have someone for you to look at," she said as she opened the back door. I knew he was in bad shape as he tumbled out, and I could feel the vomit surge hot in my throat as I caught that first glimpse of his leg: skin burned charcoal black, bone exposed, nothing even still alive enough to bleed.

I knew this man. At least, I thought I did. As the village drunk of Masese, he was a constant annoyance to me when Amazima carried out ministry there. He would stumble, swearing, through my Bible study as our group met outside and bang on my car windows as I drove through the community. I was appalled but not surprised to learn that while he was passed out in the middle of the day, a lantern tipped over and caught his house on fire. The fire also caught his leg, waking him, and he crawled out just in time to watch his neighbors steal his few unburned belongings from inside.

Again I wondered, *Really, God? Do you have beauty here?* And thus began the season that I thought would heal him but instead healed me.

Christine and I took him straight to the local hospital, where doctors shook their heads in disbelief. Nobody had the time or resources to deal with this. Antibiotics and clean dressings were expensive and hard to come by there. The nurses were overworked and understaffed, doing their best to serve wards of twenty to forty patients alone.

"We have a few choices," explained the doctor. "We can amputate, or someone can dress it daily. I don't know if my nurses will have the time, but I can show you how."

I nodded, hesitant.

"If you don't, he will lose this leg. He might lose it anyway."

Something in me that I could not yet name rose up to fight. It wasn't fair for this man to lose his leg. As I look back, I think I just could not stand the idea of another loss of this magnitude so soon after our family had experienced the great loss of Jane's presence in our home. Although I had no idea at the time, Jesus was bringing about my own healing by drawing me into someone else's. I couldn't verbalize it then, but it was as if my heart screamed, *I lost my daughter. I lost a part of my heart. You will* not *lose your leg! Not on my watch.* And so I observed and learned as the doctor taught me exactly what to do to give Mack's leg the best chance of survival.

The thoughts of *not enough* crept in. How would I possibly add another task to my already-full days? I remembered the trust of the widow of Zarephath, how God had taken her meager offering of a lump of flour and had it made *enough.* He would take my offering of obedience and timid trust and make it enough here. *Be faithful with the little you have,* He whispered again.

As we arrived home, I did my best to explain to Mack what was going on. Still drunk, he moaned and mumbled a story I couldn't understand. I prayed over his wound and over his heart, and when he fell asleep on the porch, I didn't make him move but draped a blanket over him. I didn't realize this simple action would be the beginning of my coming to love the newest, most unconventional member of our family.

For a month Mack came and went. I bandaged the leg every day and sent him home; then Christine would pick him up from his half-burned-down hut the next day. And I would be almost thankful that he was drunk, because even still his pain was excruciating.

For nearly an hour each day I scraped the dead skin from this wound, and God scraped at the dead places of my heart. Buried places that, though I would never say it aloud, somehow still doubted that God could be good, all the time, when Jane's bed lay empty. As I scraped at that wound in silence, I internally asked all the hard questions. Then I said it out loud, to Mack and to myself. "God uses all for good. For His glory. God is using this," I said, and I smiled when new pink life began showing around his wound. Though I didn't recognize it yet, God also was growing new life in the very hardest places of my heart as I learned to trust Him more and more.

I wrote blessings on sticky notes and helped children with homework and read everything about wound care I could get my hands on. I got to know so many wonderful nurses in the area who would come and help me, showing me things I didn't know. God always sent just the right people at just the right times, again amazing me with His provision. I washed and scraped and scrubbed and dressed and cried, and I said to that wound and to anyone who would listen, "We will not lose this leg."

Others from the community stepped over our new friend as he lay asleep on the porch and they shook their heads. "You can't save 'em all. Not this one, Katie." But I was stubborn. And God was relentless.

Eventually, Mack moved into the little three-room house in our backyard. Christine often had trouble finding him in the community, as he would wander in his drunken stupor, and we couldn't risk infection in his leg. Moving him in made finding him at bandaging time quite a bit easier, and it allowed me to make sure he wasn't drinking, as he remained safely behind our locked gate most of the time. As he began to sober up, we dove into longer conversations. He told me all about his life and his family before he became an alcoholic and homeless in Masese. He told me of the loss of his father and then his mother and then each of his brothers one by one, that once he had no one left, his loneliness overwhelmed him and he had no reason to stop drinking. He told me of how his addiction slowly became something he couldn't control, so he had dropped out of college with only one year left and began consuming so much alcohol that he could no longer hold down a job. He explained that the drinking masked his hunger so that he didn't have to dig through the trash for something to eat.

I assured him that he wasn't alone. I told him about a Savior born as an infant in a feeding trough and nailed to a tree, God's provision, His promised Lamb. I told him of a Body broken for him and for me and for each one of us, and I didn't even realize as I spoke that my tears were pooling on the cement porch. I sat astonished that messy, inadequate me would get to share such a story. In truth, I needed to be assured of those promises just as much as he did.

He questioned everything I said about God's goodness and sovereignty, and without knowing it, as I answered him, I answered myself too. In the darkest place of my life, as I mourned Jane's absence and precarious future, God had me testify each day about exactly who I knew Him to be. In my head, I knew who God was, but with Mack, just knowing wasn't enough. I had to speak it aloud to him over and over. I had to explain myself. And as I testified, I believed it all the more. In those hours of wound bandaging, He was introducing Himself to me *again*. The Working All for Good God. The Still and Always Faithful God. The Lord Who Will Provide. The God who sees who we are and uses all the broken places to make us who we are becoming. I named out loud the things I knew to be true of my Savior, and I watched God make them true all over again.

After 252 days of wrapping and talking and laughing and crying, new skin covered the once-dead area, and Mack's leg was almost completely healed. The leg so many believed to be a lost cause could now walk and even run. And the man so many thought was hopeless had been sober for more than six months.

A week later, this physically healed man walked into my kitchen and grinned from ear to ear. "I believe it," he announced. "Today I believe that Jesus is the Son of God." Simple as that.

I didn't try to contain my excitement as I danced around the kitchen that day, and I continued to choke back tears as the time I once spent wrapping his leg in gauze instead was spent scouring the Bible with Mack for the answers to his every question. In time I connected Mack to a male friend in our community who could continue to disciple and teach him as his love for the Word grew. God's glory and goodness were so very apparent in the transformation of this man's life.

We've been wounded. We all have. Mack and I, we both walk with a limp. His is more visible than mine, but like Jacob, we walk limping and with new and greater understanding of our Father God. In the wounding, He has changed us, renamed us. He redefined redemption and beauty for me not as a happy ending but as His presence with me, regardless of the ending. In Mack's story, I get to see it. Other times, I don't. But even then I know certainly that I can trust Him. I give Him my little and He makes up for my lack. I surrender and watch Him pour out His provision, even if that provision looks different from what I expected.

Years later we will sit around our dining room table and eat meatballs to celebrate his birthday, and he will tell us of his new home and his new job and all the Lord is doing in his life. I will think of how God has healed that hole in Mack's leg and in his life, and I will think of Jane. Her living situation remains unstable, her future a question mark. I am not sure I can fully see beauty or redemption. I am not sure I ever will. I still hear her laughter. I hear that giggle that I cannot capture in words on this page, a sound that rings in my ears. I see her deep dimples as I grab her close. And I still don't know how I feel about the way this story ended, how I would explain to someone else the mark her situation has left on my heart. Perhaps I would say humbly that I trust God so much that I would write the story the same because of all He taught me and all the ways He grew me and all that I know of Him now because of those long nights of tears and those walls lined with sticky notes of thanksgiving. Or perhaps I would clutch my hands tight and look at Jane's life now and still say, "No, God, this can't be good, and no, I wouldn't write the story this way. In my version, it would end *better*."

But one thing I do know. In the wrestling, He makes us who we are meant to be in Him. It isn't easy and it isn't pain free, but it can be glorious. In the wrestling, we get to be right up next to our strong Father and tangibly know the truth that He does not let go. He will not let go. We walk wounded, like Jacob, but we have seen the face of God in our pain, and we have encountered a new kind of intimacy with the One who holds our hearts in His. We might walk away scarred, but we are stronger and we are renamed: *His.*

Sometimes on days when I need reminding, I ask Mack, "Can I look at your leg?" He knows why I want to see. He will roll his baggy pants up to his knee, chuckle, and say, "See what God did?" The burned area is still a few shades lighter than the skin surrounding it. We both look at that leg and see so much more than new skin.

We see Jesus.

He met us right there on the cold, hard cement floor of my sunroom with our festering wounds and our messy hearts. He took two broken people and showed us the scars on His hands and whispered that it was okay if we had our scars too, because the scars were always meant to draw us into His glory.

5

PRISONERS OF HOPE

THE SUNFLOWERS ARE GROWN NOW. At least ten feet tall and radiant, they lift their faces to the sun. I watch them through the kitchen window, and a memory flashes through my mind of children with cabbage leaves on their heads and dirt under their fingernails.

I think of the words of Proverbs that had caught my eye earlier this morning as I sipped coffee in the still-quiet house before life began: "To the hungry even what is bitter tastes sweet."[1] Could it be?

This is what He had been teaching me, even though I didn't have the words yet. When I hunger always for Him, even the hard satisfies. Even the grief gives way to joy. Even the bitter is sweet. Even in the dark, I can see His face. Because when we are looking for Him, *we will always see Him*. I have tasted of His goodness, and now I hunger for it.

I need to be reminded of this daily, and in His grace, He has given me children as the greatest reminder. Parenting people from broken places makes our own brokenness all the more evident. All the questions and fears and second-guessing of God's goodness and love that we bury—because *who would speak that out loud?*—are right on the surface for children who have known a lifetime of pain in a few short years and have already wrestled with all the adult questions. God knit our family together from many different places, and our hurts are on display quite often, surfacing at different times and in different circumstances. I wonder routinely if He chose the right person to tend to all these precious hearts while He is still so clearly working on my own.

On this particular morning there is much to be thankful for. Mack, raking leaves, walks by and waves as I continue looking out the window. His leg is healed now, and he has found a job in town as a dental assistant. He is saving money so that he can move out into a small apartment we have found down the road, and he jumps at any opportunity to help our family, taking out the trash and cleaning the yard routinely. I smile and wave back. *Every bitter thing is sweet,* I think as I thank God for the sweetness of this friendship. Chaos erupts behind me, and I turn to see a daughter running to me in tears.

After years of uncertainty in her early life, not knowing what to expect or who to trust, not knowing if she would, in fact, be fed and safe from one day to the next, even the most minor change of plans rocks this ten-year-old's entire world.

"You said we could go to the pool today!" she wails. "But Agnes just said we are going tomorrow."

I can't remember what I'd said. My attempts at explanations and reasoning only make her cries grow louder. Finally, she collapses into a puddle on the floor, kicking and writhing in protest. Frustration wells up in me at how something so minor could cause such an enormous reaction, and I shout harshly, "If you're going to react like that, go to your room!" Immediately, I regret my tone. I see the sting of my words in her eyes for a fleeting moment, and then her fit intensifies all the more. How can a morning unravel so fast?

I stand there in the kitchen, my inadequacy exposed. Her unwarranted response comes from years of trauma; mine comes from irritation and, well, sin. I chastise myself for losing my temper, for not giving her the consistently calm response she needs.

As I'm tempted to wallow in guilt over all that I am *not* for my children, gently He points out that I was never meant to meet all their needs anyway. It isn't me who can make up for all their losses and hurts. He reminds me that I cannot be what they need Him to be: Savior. I quietly beg Him to fill in the gaps. Really, we are all crying out for the exact same thing: a true and consistent love that does not waver, a Savior who comes and binds up our wounds. Really, her heart is crying out for the exact thing I need myself, only her needs present on the surface, and mine are buried beneath a veil of performance, perfectionism, and pride. Hers come out messy and honest and desperate, and mine come out polished and deceiving and casual, as if I, too, am not craving a great rescue. I have so much to learn.

Nearly five years ago, this same child had bounded into my life in a dress with a bright-red sash. She tentatively called me Mommy after having not known one for nearly her entire five years of life. Initially, most signs of trauma were quickly masked with little girls' songs and dances and giggles as she adjusted to life in a family. I see that little girl, so thirsty for affection and desperate to know she is seen and loved exactly as she is, and I wonder if she could ever truly know the love I feel for her, so deep that it aches in the best of ways.

A few years after she joined our family, I watched her feet run in bright-red sneakers toward the towering swing set. The trauma that had

once been masked now surfaced in many different ways. We had struggled for joy and slowly we were finding it; she had thrashed against love
and, by God's grace, I was learning to hold on tight. She pretended to fly
on the swings, and I just knew she would soar in life. Philippians 1:6
became my daily prayer for her, for each of my girls: "being confident of
this: that he who began a good work in you will carry it on to completion
until the day of Christ Jesus."

It broke me how hard life was for this little one. For years, she struggled to receive affection and to trust that it would not be taken away; in
fact, she often pushed against affection to protect herself from the inevitable hurt it might cause if it was taken away. Some days she kicked and
screamed and did the unspeakable. But when logic said that I should be
angry or might love her less, my desire for her was only stronger. And as
I saw the extent of her brokenness and mine, I loved her even more.

Recently, red beads at the end of her braids clicked around her face
as she skipped into the kitchen to find her head a resting place on my
shoulder, now so tall she barely needed to reach up. She whispered of the
wounds once covered but never healed, and my heart broke. No child
should go through what she had endured—the pain she was still trying
to process. Although I was thankful for the words she shared with me,
an unfamiliar panic crept up the back of my throat and settled in as it hit
me, the full weight of how much we had yet to overcome. I took her face
in my hands and through blurred eyes assured her, assured myself, that
Jesus had thought of her and her red beads and her red sash even as His
red blood spilled out to redeem us all, and because I knew that, I knew
this: He would not leave us here.

～

Months later on a Tuesday in the still-dark house, I drank too-strong
coffee and I drank of His grace. I prayed over my daughter, a splash of

red in the tapestry of our family: feisty, powerful, full of care, and wielding unlimited capacity for compassion. I wrestled with "what if" and "if only," then released those questions to God's sovereignty, again. I wasn't really reading Zechariah, more just aimlessly flipping through my Bible, but then it jumped out at me. Right there on the worn pages, I read where Zechariah called God's people "prisoners of hope."[2] I knew that I hadn't been. Once more I had become captured by overwhelming concern about the trauma of my children's pasts and shifted my gaze away from what, from whom, I was meant to be captive to.

Wanting a deeper understanding of how it might look to be a prisoner of hope, I turned back to the first chapter of Zechariah and started reading. As I turned the pages, I couldn't stop underlining *everything* as my soul cried out "Yes!" to these truths. "I am coming, and I will live among you," declares the God of the Old Testament to the prophet long before He sends His Son. "Many nations will be joined with the LORD in that day and will become my people."[3] The next chapter describes a vision in which the high priest Joshua stands in front of the Lord, Satan the accuser, and the angel of the Lord. The Lord rebukes Satan for his accusations against the high priest and calls Joshua "a burning stick snatched from the fire."[4] And aren't we all? What unmatched, unmerited kindness from God that He Himself has snatched us from the fire of judgment! How much more will He redeem us from our struggles in this temporary life if He has snatched us from the fire for all eternity? I see members of my family, each from our own places, with our different backgrounds and our different hurts, snatched from the fire of certain death and brought into His safety and grace.

Then right there in front of the Lord and the angel of the Lord, Joshua's filthy clothes are removed and he is clothed in fine garments and a clean turban, and the Lord promises, "I am going to bring my servant, the Branch."[5]

As I read this, I remember how Isaiah spoke of a Branch that would bear fruit, a shoot that would grow forth from a dead stump.[6] Is this hope? That we could look at a stump, long dead and lifeless, and expect a shoot where it would presumably be impossible? That we can look at our hopeless situations, seemingly dead—a child unable to attach, a prodigal who has lost her way, a marriage beyond repair, a jobless, homeless drug addict who craves a fix more than a Savior—and expect new life to shoot forth? What the world would call foolishness, to look at a stump and expect a branch, is what the Lord has for us in Jesus. As I consider this, my mind and my heart fill with the promises that He has given me for my children over the years, one in particular that keeps coming back: "They will be called oaks of righteousness, a planting of the LORD for the display of his splendor."[7]

We look for Jesus, who bestows on us "a crown of beauty instead of ashes, the oil of gladness instead of mourning, and a garment of praise instead of a spirit of despair";[8] Jesus, who removes our filthy clothes and replaces them with fine garments, taking away all our sin; Jesus, who comes for His bride and gives her fine linen, bright and clean to wear.[9] To be a prisoner of hope is to be the freest of all because we look at our circumstances and expect Jesus to enter in and redeem, renew, restore.

> In him it has always been "Yes." For no matter how many promises God has made, they are "Yes" in Christ . . . [because] he anointed us, set his seal of ownership on us, and put his Spirit in our hearts as a deposit, guaranteeing what is to come. . . . Therefore, since we have such a *hope,* we are very bold."[10]

Hope is my captor: hope for my daughter's healing here (which has already begun), hope for the healing of my own broken places, and hope for our lives eternal with Him. Hope that, as Philippians 1:6 says, He who began a good work in us is not finished yet and will carry it to completion until the day that He comes. And I am a prisoner to the hope that *He is coming*.

The sun peeks over the horizon and dances patterns across the couch. I see with new eyes, a captive of the hope set fully on the grace given me through Christ. I must live my days as this kind of prisoner because true freedom is found only in being completely captivated by a coming King.

This child over whom I've been praying, who is always the first one awake, pulls a book off the shelf and snuggles up next to me in silence, her ten-year-old lankiness curling up like an infant inside waiting arms. I see hope in her, and I see myself. I, too, can kick and scream and thrash hard against the Father's love. I shift my focus and become a prisoner to the panic instead of the promise, and still He says, "Mine." He looks at me, broken, and calls me daughter and ever so lovingly pulls me right back in.

I study her face and can't imagine that I know only a fraction of His love for her as I whisper the prayers of every morning over her heart: "Jesus, You bind up the brokenhearted . . . set the captives free . . . comfort those who mourn . . . bestow beauty instead of ashes . . . They will be called oaks of righteousness, a display of the Lord's splendor."[11] I trace the curve of her face with my fingers and praise the Lord for such resilience and transformation as I have seen in this child. I praise Him for her salvation and the way she is hungrily learning more about Him each day.

And then I write small, on her hand and mine, *Prisoner of hope*.

I want to live as a prisoner to the yes, this great expectancy that we will see Jesus here. Remembering all we have seen, we set our hope fully on what we have not yet seen. We place all our hope and all our trust and all our focus on the grace given us through Christ, and we beg to live captured by His promises.

Parenting has undoubtedly been my greatest teacher of God's love for me. By His grace, He created me in a way that reaching into the brokenness of others is not terribly uncomfortable for me. But I find that being broken, having brokenness in my home when I feel that I should be able to control and fix things, is much more difficult. Maybe that's true for all of us. In loving our very own, we display to them the weaknesses we'd rather conceal, brokenness that we can hide from the rest of the world but not from our families.

As time passes, I realize more and more how conditioned I have been to be ashamed of my weakness. Somehow it is okay to attend to the brokenness in the lives of others, but to admit to brokenness in our own homes, even in our own hearts? We have been told that this is downright embarrassing. What we know to be true, though, as we dig into Scripture, is that God is not ashamed of our weakness. He is not ashamed of it, because He can use even this to glorify Himself.

I think of Mary of Bethany, her tears mixed with perfume washing the dusty feet of Jesus. This place we are trained to run from—vulnerability—is so precious and beautiful to Him. My inability to fill my children's heart holes puts me in a place of need. And my need for Jesus is beautiful to Him; it is what He wants. This lack that the world would call "bitter" is sweet to my Savior as it draws me into dependence on and relationship with Him.

My lack is evident in my children's tears over let-down expectations, a voice raised in frustration in response to a simple request, my failure to understand how being asked to sweep up a few piles could so suddenly send someone into an utter meltdown, the ways I lie awake in worry and fear, trying to control my children's stories and the journeys that they are on. One child screams at me that I didn't do this or that and I've let her down, and I stare, blinking, not really sure what she is even talking about. For this one, with her beautiful sensitive heart that bears too many wounds of the past, just a wrong glance or careless word cuts deep and reminds her of the ways she's been cast aside. I know this and yet at times still am heedless of causing hurt. My weakness is so evident. I humble myself and apologize, and I thank God for how He is working in us all.

Later in the day, I hear echoes of jealousy, insecurity, competition, and complaints of unfairness among them—who is loved more or who received less. Another child cries over the sting of someone's words and I cry harder, feeling her hurt, feeling that I have failed to protect her little heart.

All these hearts and all these personalities, just like any family. You and I both know the truth of it: loving people is hard. It brings us to the very end of ourselves. And as much as we are trained to avoid it, the end of ourselves is such a very sweet place to be. The truth rings as clearly as it does for Mary in that moment at His feet: I am not sufficient. My parenting cannot be sufficient. Only He is sufficient and only He can fill up these holes, for all of us.

In those early years of God knitting our hearts together, to an outsider or really anyone with little experience of adoption, I am sure we looked like a broken-down mess of a family—the very kind of wrecked and damaged that some people spend their whole lives trying to avoid.

Sometimes I would rush down the driveway in our only vehicle, a sixteen-passenger van, and I would get out and life would be so obviously beautiful. Daughters would greet me laughingly at the gate. I'd step into our home and there would be the smell of fresh wheat bread baking in the oven, bread I had put in before I left. Later on, there would be a long run at nap time and clean laundry on the line and thirteen bodies piled together with me on the couch before bed. With a large family, these days are the definition of miraculous.

But more often, life was messy. There were daughters at the gate, but they were bickering with each other. The people living with our family might be untidy and intrusive, and they would see our not-good selves, and I didn't want to bake the bread because today I *just wanted to go to sleep* and wake up when this mess was over.

We enjoyed seasons of peace and cuddling and reading aloud on the couch and dinner on time and all things going smoothly. We endured seasons when one person's wailing threw the whole family off track and I would wonder what I was doing in this role of parenting and if we would ever get back on track.

These weak and ruined days pushed me closer to Him. There were no parenting books for our kind of family, no one specific strategy that would heal all the wounds and tend all the hearts. There was only Jesus, and I leaned into Him more and more to learn how to answer such a seemingly impossible call. It was only when I acknowledged my weakness and called out in my deep need for Him that I really had any answers. As I leaned into Him, He caught and equipped me. And there was no way to possibly think that this strength could come from my own self; only a strength and grace that came from Him would allow me to love my daughters well.

I witnessed the secrets He was growing on the inside, the progress He was making slowly but surely in their hearts. I saw it as they loved the people who came into our home so extravagantly and without any pretense. I saw it in the little notes they wrote me, the flowers they picked and brought in proudly, the way they desired to surprise and please their sisters on birthdays, the way they learned to say "I'm sorry" (and I did too).

I knew the secrets God was whispering to my own heart as He brought about in me a *desire* for the weak and desperate place that compelled me to pray for myself and for my children, not as a discipline but as a *lifeline*. No amount of organization or planning or parenting goals could get me there. A perfectly organized house and healthy home-cooked meals and impeccable lists of spelling words were not the answer. Tired, needy, and desperate, I had only Him to cling to. And the more I knew my feebleness, my flaws, and my shortcomings, the more I knew His gentleness toward me, His tender glance, His strong and loving shoulder that was always available to lean on.

These people I loved so much that I could feel the physical ache in my chest, He was using them then, and still is, to transform me—to transform my view of both myself and Him. These children are my very most challenging, and very best, task.

The Branch is for me too. I wait expectantly for healing not only in my daughters but also in my own heart as my weakness ushers me closer and closer to Him. *Prisoners of hope,* He whispers to my heart, *are those who look at a stump and expect a shoot, look at the desert and expect a mighty oak tree, look at their circumstances and expect the Branch, Jesus.*

6

WE HAVE
ONE ANOTHER

OUR VAN PULLS INTO THE bumpy dirt space next to her crusted
dirt house in the dusty, overcrowded slum, and there she stands, her
smile like sunshine. It is hot and we are late, but her joy reminds me of
where I find my joy. My two youngest see her and clap and chant, grin-
ning, "Miss Angelina, Miss Angelina!"

Her hug is warm and encouraging like a mother's, and I rest there a
moment. "Good morning, sweet friend," I say. The word *friend* rolls off
my tongue and fills up my heart as my children pull on her skirt and
crawl up into her arms, because *friend* is the word that captures who she
is to all of us. She herds the girls into her house no bigger than my
kitchen, where she has tea and biscuits waiting for them. A snack so
simple is, for her, a sacrifice. I am humbled. I have to run down the hill
and start Bible study, but the girls don't bat an eye. They know they are
safe here. "They'll stay here with me," she says, chuckling. "Enjoy your
meeting." I thank her and whisper more thanks as I walk away down the

hill. The full weight of it hits me again: here in the most unlikely of places and circumstances, this woman has become my friend.

Masese is a slum community of about five thousand people, perched on a hillside on the outskirts of the bustling town of Jinja. On the other side of the same hill is the town's landfill, where many of Masese's inhabitants find their livelihood by picking through the trash for scraps of metal to sell or food to eat. Those who do not engage in this work often turn to brewing alcohol or prostitution to support themselves and their families. Poverty, hunger, disease, and alcohol addiction are rampant here. There is beauty here too, though, as children laugh and dance, undeterred by the red dust swirling all around them, as women invite in their neighbors and look out for one another's children and share the little they have. After my years of ministry in this community, I've begun to think of it as a second home, with people like Angelina readily welcoming our family.

Weeks later, Santina, another friend from this same small community, lets me put my hand on her shoulder and hold her child as she bends her head to weep. I had witnessed the birth of this child in this same tiny mud hut a couple years ago. There was no power here, so we had stood in the dim light of a candle, waiting until her mother delivered her with one loud cry. Before I knew it, someone had placed the baby, still vernix covered and slippery, in my lap as the other women went about helping Santina deliver the placenta and get cleaned up. I remember how the baby didn't really cry, more just squeaked, and her curious eyes had stared up at me in the dark house. I wrapped her in the nearest cloth I could find, and they named her Katie. Now today, Katie's father had gasped his last breath and closed his eyes in death as I held him in the very same lap that once held her wriggling new life. My head whirls as I consider how life and death tangle together, how we can rarely anticipate what a new day might bring. Because there is little I can offer besides my presence and words of comfort, I mop Santina's tiny house.

Later, I stand with their family in the rain and we cry. She has seven children, four of whom were with us when their father died. Neighbors come to mourn with the family, and I feel their reassuring hands on my shoulders. An onlooker might think that I should be afraid here, in the slum, in the dark middle of the night, in the rain—and maybe once I would have been—but I feel only comfort. This place has become a kind of sanctuary for me. I have found friends here. I have found fellowship. Mack stands with us too, having driven my van here so that I could sit in the back seat to hold and comfort Santina's little ones. Really, I think he just didn't want me to go alone. This is where he once lived, before the accident, before he moved into our backyard. He doesn't let me stray far from his sight, my faithful guardian. He is protective of me, like a brother, and because he is concerned for my grief, he stays near. Dozens of faces reflect in the candlelight as we crowd into Santina's tiny home, and I marvel at how the same people who used to spit at me because of the color of my skin now join hands with mine in the night. "Thank you for crying for our pain," Lillian says, and words fail me.

I remember that theologian Henri Nouwen wrote,

> [Compassion] is not a bending toward the underprivileged from a
> privileged position; it is not a reaching out from on high to those
> who are less fortunate below; it is not a gesture of sympathy or
> pity for those who fail to make it in the upward pull. On the
> contrary, compassion means going directly to those people and
> places where suffering is most acute and building a home there.[1]

And so we sit.

This is what I want for our lives, mine and my children. Not to pity but to suffer with these people. To walk alongside. To build our home in community with them. To share in their burdens.

I walk back up the muddy hill, my path lit dimly by the lantern of a nearby chapati stand. The village is crowded, people living in rickety shacks packed tightly into one small area. As I walk, I can't help but bump into people I know, and we embrace in the night. Even on these hardest days I feel gratitude because I know this: These people, they are my friends. God has made it true that my joy is their joy and their pain is my pain. In this unlikely place, He has made relationship beautiful.

Weeks later, a group of women from this same slum sit in a circle in my yard, where we have gathered for Bible study. I serve tea and paint their toenails and our laughter is real. We read the Word and share prayer requests and praises. Not all of them believe yet, but they are starting to recognize His answers, to see that our prayers are real too. We have laughed at our days and cried for our sorrows. We have grieved death and rejoiced in new life. We have shared wild stories, and we have sat in the silence. And despite a million differences, we are really all just the same, one people bonded by relationship.

Though Namele is part of this same group of women that gathers each Tuesday, we can hardly understand each other. I speak English and Luganda. Namele speaks Nkarimojong and Swahili. At Bible study, we use a translator, but today she has come to me for help because her baby is sick. With no one here who can really speak her language, I can't figure out how in the world she is going to tell me what is wrong. I try all kinds of crazy sign language. She just stares at me.

I start making gagging noises, as if I am going to vomit.

She nods her head enthusiastically.

"How many times?" I ask and even try to sign.

She doesn't get it.

I make the vomiting sound once; she shakes her head no. I make it twice. I make it three times. On the fourth, she nods her head earnestly again. We stare at each other.

And then we fall to the floor in stitches. We both realize how ridiculous this is.

The baby has a fever, so I hand Namele some medicine. She smiles, but when I stand up to go, she pulls me back onto the couch. *"Eklip,"* she says, and I know that one. Pray. She wants me to pray for her baby. My heart dips because I know she has seen too much, enough that a fever can send a mother's heart into fear for the life of her child. She lives where malnutrition and disease, lack of clean water and unsanitary conditions put her children at risk every day, and just as any other mother would, she prays that her baby will be healthy and safe. Though communication is difficult between us, I have seen her eagerness for the Word, her faith in trials, her joy in knowing Jesus. I curl myself back up next to her on the couch and I thank Jesus for Namele and for her baby boy and for His love. She lays her little one on the couch asleep and stays for dinner. And as she sits at my table and holds my hand as we bow our heads in prayer again, joy floods over me. Though we struggle through communication barriers and cultural differences, this woman is my friend.

German pastor Dietrich Bonhoeffer wrote that our community with one another consists solely in what Christ has done for all of us.

> I have community with others and will continue to have it
> only through Jesus Christ. The more genuine and the deeper
> our community becomes, the more everything else between
> us will recede, and the more clearly and purely will Jesus
> Christ and his work become the one and only thing that is
> alive between us. We have one another only through Christ,
> but through Christ we do *have* one another . . . completely
> and for all eternity.[2]

What a beautiful promise!

Status, culture, and language mean nothing in light of eternity. Race, age, and life experiences fade away. Namele's hand is in mine and we bow to our Creator and we break bread and we laugh. Oh, we laugh. I hold her baby and she holds mine and we care about each other in a way that is real and deep. She sits on my couch or I sit on her dirt floor and we exchange a few words that we can both understand in broken verb tenses. We love, and it is enough. And it will remain true for all eternity.

Years ago I began to pray over all those God brought into our home a prayer I had often whispered to Him in regard to my daughters: "Father, give me Your eyes for them. Give me your eyes for this man, this woman, this child. Show me how You see each one." And without a doubt, though not always immediately, God answers a prayer such as this. Does He not long for us to receive one another, to love one another, to care for one another, in the same way He cares for them? Does He not want us to see each other with new eyes and new hearts?

And if compassion truly means to suffer with, then seeing our visitors with new eyes, being compassionate as He is compassionate, is not to pity, not to extend a hand of charity, but to be truly broken, to feel gut-wrenching pain when we see others suffer. In this way, maybe we are not called to alleviate suffering (as I had once imagined) as much as we are called to enter into the suffering of others and walk with them through it. We mourn with those who mourn, we weep with those who weep, we cry out with them for something better.

My Western ideals of ministry and even missionary work would have, at one time, kept a separation between personal life and ministry, between home and work. But the longer our family abides with and among others who are more materially needy, but truly only just as des-

perate for Christ as we are, the more this separation seems not only un-
biblical but impossible. Life was certainly intended to be lived as ongoing
ministry, not separate from ministry. Of course, the more I asked my
Father God to give me His eyes for the people He brought into our life
and home, the more He confirmed that He did not view anyone as the
next ministry project or person to be evangelized but as someone just like
me who needed to be lavished with His undeserved, unmerited blessing,
love, and favor. He was changing my vision, again giving me eyes to see
that we most deeply experience His beauty when we walk with others in
the darkness.

"We loved you so much that we were delighted to share with you not
only the gospel of God but our lives as well," wrote Paul, Silas, and Timo-
thy to the church at Thessalonica.[3] This resonated deeply with my spirit
as all different kinds of people made their home in and around our house.
I wanted to live this every day of our lives! I wanted people to understand
the Gospel not because of our words but because of the way we lived.

This lifestyle of sharing and inviting others in—to sit at our tables,
rest on our couches, shower in our bathrooms, and sleep in our beds—
goes against everything Western culture teaches about valuing personal
space and privacy. With all these extra people, quiet and personal space
were things of the past. I used to find it inconvenient, disruptive, even
uncomfortable. But God continued to stretch me more and more and to
teach me that this interruptible, public lifestyle is the way He desires me
to live and to love. So we made a conscious decision as a family to welcome all to our table. I began to practice the art of being interrupted. As
I chopped pounds and pounds of vegetables, I prayed that people would
be not only filled physically at my table but also filled spiritually in our
home. And as my heart cried out for this to be true, God continued to
give us opportunities to live in this way.

Katherine was a young widowed mother of five children under the age of ten and one young woman already grown. Most of her children were in Amazima's sponsorship program, receiving financial support for their education and medical care. Katherine had been fighting tuberculosis, a complication from HIV, for a while, but recently it had gotten bad enough that she was rapidly losing weight and had very little energy. I got a call from one of our staff members, who worried that Katherine might not be strong enough to take care of herself or her children or to make the weekly trek from her village to the hospital in town where she was receiving her treatment. With the room in the backyard next to Mack's vacant, it seemed like a no-brainer to invite them to come stay. Katherine didn't need much, just some good food and a little extra care; I figured it would be a month, maybe two, before she was strong and healthy enough to move out and care for her children on her own again.

Our family welcomed theirs and we became fast friends. Katherine was stubborn, like me, and she wanted the best for her kids, even though she wasn't currently strong enough to make it happen. She had an opinion about everything and readily made it known as the rest of us bustled about trying to ensure she got the very best care possible. She took her medicine and got some rest and ate nutritious food while her two oldest, Edith and Penny, came to be homeschooled with my kindergartners, and her little guys ran around the backyard. Friends turned into family as we adjusted to life with six more people.

It is a bit of a mess, this business of love. As more and more people enter our lives, we are left with no choice but to enter theirs as well. Even more so, over time their pains become our pain and their joys become our joy and this sharing of the Gospel becomes a sharing of life. This, at first glance, seems so burdensome, so overwhelming, but somehow I have found it not to be any longer. Something about shouldering the burdens of another brings a lightness to our own affliction. We are in it together, and Christ is in it with us.

The world would like to tell us otherwise; the world would teach us that pain is what ruins us. We are trained and conditioned to run from pain at all costs. Some would even argue that doing so is primal instinct. Only the supernatural working of the Holy Spirit can override this fear of pain with a love that is greater. The world would teach us that once we are broken, we cannot be used, we cannot be strong, we cannot be happy. But this is not true. In the very greatest miracle of all time, our Father God resurrects His Son Jesus out of the dark tomb and conquers death. After the brutal beating and scourging and mocking that is a direct result of the ugliness of my sin, Jesus whispers, "Father, forgive them." And He does. Out of the black of the tomb, new Life emerges and new Light shines forth. The Lamb, the Lamb. God uses all things, even pain, for His glory.

This is what I saw Him doing in our home, even before I could express my great desire for it. This is what I long for Him to continue in our home today. As He does, He teaches me to view pain as a holy invitation to know Him more so that I can share Him more. Again and again, Jesus renews in me a desire to live this way, a desire to minister this way, a desire to mother this way.

This desire to see all people as He sees them, to do life and death and joy and pain as one with our neighbor, has defined our family's entire lifestyle. Simple things like throwing a birthday party for someone who otherwise wouldn't have one or making a meal to share with a patient in the local hospital, stopping to look into a tired mother's eyes and listen as she speaks of her struggles or squeezing an extra space around the table for a hungry passerby—these things let others know that we are with them and for them and that God is with them and for them too.

Jesus set aside all my original plans and dreams for how I would change communities and lives in Uganda. This place and these people, He uses them to change and shape *me*. I share with them so little, and they share with me wisdom and joy and laughter. They let me sit with them and listen to their stories and their wisdom. They let me experience God's goodness and redemption in their painful circumstances. They embody genuine hospitality even at the price of sacrifice, and they teach me true gratitude even in the face of poverty. As I sit with them, as I learn from them, I know God's goodness in new ways.

7

A Dry and Weary Land

THE MONTHS PASSED AND KATHERINE wasn't getting better. We continued to follow all the doctors' instructions, and they assured us we were doing everything we could to address the symptoms of her advanced illness. Still, everyone agreed that her disease had progressed too far for her body to fight much longer. We discussed hospice care, but I did not want to believe that we were out of options. She had five little children, all happy and healthy and leaping around my living room. Surely, she just had to get better and they would move back to their home, restored to the happy, healthy family they once were. She was so young. Her children were so young, so in need of their mother.

I remember sitting on the side of her bed, like I did every morning, to ensure that she was swallowing down the drugs meant to make her better but that also made her feel nauseous. We spoke about the option of a possible surgery and all it would entail as well as the idea of simply resigning to palliative care and doing the best we could with what we had left. I knew the prognosis. I had seen the doctor's most recent report and knew his speech before he gave it—that the antiretroviral drugs meant to save her life were tearing her stomach apart and that eighty pounds was just too small for a woman of nearly six feet. It was possible, however, that with consistent treatment and a healthy diet, something might shift and her body might start responding. This was rare, but it was possible.

"So these are your treatment options . . ." I choked back a sob. How would I present a thirty-year-old mother of five with the fact that we'd probably already done almost all we could do? "I will support you, whatever you choose." I turned so she wouldn't see me blink back the tears.

Her answer was so simple.

"I would like to choose life." Her words were steady, certain. "My children are still so young. I would like to live."

Of course. The tears burned hot in the back of my eyes, but I tried desperately not to let them fall. Not yet. It wasn't over yet.

"Yes, dear friend," I whispered. "Yes, I want you to live."

Intellectually, I knew that the chances of her improving significantly were not great. But in my heart, I knew the God of the impossible. I knew the Life Giver. I couldn't help but hope, and I asked it, *begged it,* over and over again, *Oh, Lord, might she live?* I remembered the expectancy that He had been teaching me for years, to look at the broken places and expect that He would bring beauty, to look at bleak situations and expect that He would meet us there. *The Lord Will Provide,* I told myself, and I thought of the ram in the thicket. So I looked at illness that screamed of death, and I fully expected a miracle, healing, health, life.

Sometimes His provision is so much different from what we have expected.

I read that same night of the few men in Luke carrying their paralyzed friend on a mat, desperate to lay him at the feet of Jesus. I thought of how cumbersome it must have been to hoist him up on that roof, how difficult it must have been to remove the tiles so that they could lower him through the ceiling into the middle of the crowd, right in front of Jesus.[1] And as I looked at Katherine, I thought maybe I knew a bit of the desperation they must have felt, the urgency to get him there. I thought too of the great hope they must have had that Jesus *would* heal their friend. They must have been so certain, to go to such great lengths to get him there. My heart stirred with this kind of hope, a confidence, a certainty that God would answer us, that He would heal her. I read that because of the faith of the men, Jesus forgave their friend's sin and, for His glory alone, healed the man's legs as well, told him to get up and walk. This became my desperate, hopeful prayer for Katherine—that she would get up and walk in health for the glory of God.

I resolved that I, too, would choose life. I would choose it for her and for her children. I would choose it for me. I was determined that even when the temptation to despair was overwhelming, I would choose hope, expectantly waiting on God to save not only Katherine's soul but also her life. I would choose to believe for the victory found in Christ Jesus. I knew the God who could heal her, I desperately wanted Him to heal her, and I believed that He would.

Every night after I tucked my own children in bed, I would tuck in Katherine's children all around her. I handed her a glass of milk with her medicine, and we would watch her children's chests rise and fall with sleep as hers fought hard for breath. I would sit at her bedside with her hands in mine and squeeze my eyes tight as I brought her before Jesus. In this way, I lowered her through the roof. I begged on her behalf, on behalf of her children, that she might know Him more and that for His glory alone, He would heal her, call her to get up and walk. We waited.

Another Christmas came, marking the fifth month this family had spent with us. Because Katherine was growing weaker, we had moved her from the small house in our backyard into our living room, where I could provide more immediate assistance. Katherine slept on the couch while her children piled on mattresses on the floor, right under the glittering lights of our tree.

Before the sun rose on Christmas morning, I squeezed between a pile of children and blankets in an attempt to find some quiet time by the dim light of the Christmas tree before the bustle of the day. I remember feeling distracted. Her children all had a cough, and they breathed heavily and tossed and turned all around me.

Katherine's chest heaved and a small moan escaped her lips, and I worried. The rain pounded loudly on the tin roof, rain we needed after a longer than usual dry season. I thought briefly of how the rain might interrupt the day, all our expected guests tracking in sticky red mud, but I tried to be thankful for it nonetheless. I dreamed of Katherine's future. I dreamed of the futures of her children. I fleetingly wondered if there was a relative who would raise this brood of kids if she couldn't.

I watched them sleep and heard my precious ones begin to stir in their bedrooms, and I wondered if I could do it all again today. Could I find the strength and grace to yet again care for the children and the sick and the broken and those who would come for dinner and just all these lives with all their needs? The house was all aglow with candles lit and the lights from the tree. I reminded myself of all God's promises fulfilled in a baby, and I breathed it deep: grace.

In that moment, I felt so thankful that Jesus meets me in these squished places. In the stretched-thin places. In the squeezed-between-the-tree-and-the-kids moments. In the desperate-for-quiet-on-the-bathroom-floor-because-everywhere-else-is-full moments.

I read Luke 2. I thought of Bethlehem and how the inn had no room, and I thought of how baby Jesus's parents squeezed between the animals to place Him in a feeding trough—God in the flesh, here in our pain and our mess. The shepherds gazed in wonder, but Mary held all this wonder in the silence of her heart. I bet she dreamed of His future. I bet it was dirty and noisy, but the sky was all a-twinkle with the light of that star, the heavens bursting with God's promises all fulfilled: grace.

I looked around and I knew, again, that this is what Jesus came for. The King of the universe, who created all things, even life itself, clothed in splendor, took off His royal robes, laid aside His crown, and squeezed all the fullness of God into the womb of a woman and then into swaddling clothes in a manger. The squished places and the stretched places, the moments that are too loud and too messy and too uncertain, this is what He came for. The heartaches and the doubt and the wounds that our sin carves deep, that is why He is here. And all this life that was hanging in the balance in the dark of that morning, that is why we wait, why we celebrate. We light the candles and the tree and the house, and we cry with longing in our voices and our hearts, "Oh come, oh come, Emmanuel. Come, Lord Jesus."

And His hope surged up in me again, for her, for her life. We waited.

Christmas day was full of joy. Looking back now, it is almost surprising to me just how much joy we felt even in the midst of such difficult circumstances. It is as if God graciously allowed us to put the hard aside and just celebrate. We all went to church on Christmas morning, and I remember feeling encouraged that Katherine was strong enough to walk from the van to her seat.

Later, a turkey roasted in the oven, while we temporarily put all the extra mattresses away and moved a second dining table into our living room so that guests would have more room to sit. Between the extra table and all the friends and family members who crowded into our small house, there was hardly room to move, but we didn't mind. Mashed potatoes and green beans and pumpkin pies filled up the tables, and children ran around while grown-ups tried to have conversation above the noise. Katherine and her children had become an expected part of our family by now and joined right in the festivities.

Long after the sun had set, we all gathered around one table and lit candles on a birthday cake. The kids sang "Happy Birthday" to Jesus and squealed with delight as they blew out the candles. I sat in awe of my girls, their arms around Katherine's children, eagerly making them a part of every family tradition. Their genuine hospitality and unpretentious pleasure in including them truly blessed me. As guests left and children fell exhausted into bed, their eyes sparkling from the fullness of the day, I thanked God again for His goodness to us.

The view of our sunflowers is one of my favorite things about looking out at our backyard while I stand in the kitchen. One of our many house-guests planted them a few years ago with seeds she'd brought from her home in northern Uganda. They grow nearly ten feet tall, and they lift their faces to the sun, radiant. They are always blooming during the Christmas season here.

To my dismay, the time we get to enjoy their blossoms always seems so brief in comparison to the time we wait for them to bloom. To replant them takes days of pulling the seeds from the dead heads and drying them in the sun before carefully pushing them back into the soft rich dirt during the next rainy season. Then more weeks of waiting before we finally see some tiny green shoots. We watch as the shoots become thick stalks and climb into the sky. Then, my very favorite part, the weeks of wonder as small buds open into glorious and beautiful, large flowers. If I can't find my girls before breakfast, they are in the garden, measuring and marveling at the progress of our flowers.

But all too soon, the regal flowers bend their heads and begin to die. Something in me becomes so sad as I watch the flowers lose their splendor, but the girls aren't fazed at all. The death and drying of the sunflowers bring another exciting season: harvest.

The children rush to the backyard and let the garden's mud squish between their toes. I cringe a little as they hack the stalks down and pull off the flowers that are now bigger than their faces. Each flower yields hundreds of little seeds, and the girls grin big in the face of endless possibility. I look at my now-bare garden and feel loss, but these children of mine see great opportunity and wiggle with eager anticipation. Before they set piles aside to dry for the replanting, they grab handfuls to roast as snacks.

I think we often look at our lives and see the barren places. It seems the garden is empty, plans dead and withered, dreams laid waste. It is easy to believe the lie that the good is over and gone and maybe God is done working here, in me and in you. My children know better. And if I take the time to pause and remember, I know better too. That barren garden is ripe with opportunity and possibility, those hundreds of seeds ready to fill bellies or grow and multiply again.

Could we rejoice in the waiting? Could we believe that God, who brought Jesus out of the black of the tomb and green shoots out of the hard earth, will bring beauty out of our barren seasons? Could we know that beauty is in this whole process, the growing and the pruning and even in the waiting, not just the part with the beautiful flower?

I watch my girls hard at work in the garden. This year they have extra friends to help. They gently instruct Katherine's children in which stalks to cut down and where to set the flower heads to dry. Shells of sunflower seeds peek through their sheepish grins, and I hold my tongue as their muddy little feet pad over the just-mopped floor, their arms filled with buckets of their prized harvest.

Their smiles speak of a glory that far surpasses the beauty of the flowers. Later that day, our very living room speaks of splendor that could have been designed by only God Himself. I peek around the corner of a doorway to see ten-year-old Joyce cuddled on the couch reading a book to five-year-old David. Sumini and Edith and Penny play dolls and dress-up together, and Sumini relishes having two extra "sisters" for a time who are nearly eight, just her age. Sarah and Mary dote on little John, making sure all his needs are met. Later, Scovia, Ellie,* and Tibita, who are a bit older, lead the whole gang in an exciting game, and they call me to watch as their friends put on a show.

I watch my children reach out to these others and show deep concern for their feelings about their mother's illness and their displacement from their home. They have made it their personal mission to love these little ones for however long they are with us, opening their home and their hearts to say, "We are with you. We are for you." Without complaint, they squeeze into each other on the benches around our dinner table to make room for the five extra.

The sunflower harvest is a simple but profound reminder. The girls don't grieve the empty garden, because it gives great yield. The seeds provide snacks for weeks and plenty more for replanting. Next season, there will be even more! We will replant the seeds when the rains begin, and this time the harvest will be even greater because we will have started with more seeds. The shoots will again spring up and reach for the sky. Again they will bloom, beautiful, and again they will bow, bending low

---

* Zuula has decided to go by her middle name, Elizabeth. We call her Ellie.

to the earth and waiting for my children to run wide eyed in wonder to the harvest. And each time, we replant and rain pours and the sun scorches and God brings beauty up out of the dust.

Maybe the greatest joy isn't just in beholding the flowers but in the process. I think over the past years and all the dark and hard places. God has protected us from the pounding rain and the scorching sun, like baby green shoots clinging to Him for dear life. I think even of the pain and loss in each of my girls' stories that has grown in them such a capacity for kindness and generosity toward others and the way He is using even parts of their stories that I do not know to minister to the extras we find around our table.

As the evening wears on, I sit at the dining room table and look at them sprawled all over each other on the couches to watch a movie. Mack joins us for the movie too, and he grins at me, probably wondering why I sit where I do, watching the people instead of the film. And it is true here too: a wound all healed and covered with smooth new skin is a wonderful thing to behold but not nearly as wonderful as the friendship that was built in the tending of that wound and the waiting for it to heal.

Dreams die and seasons end and terrible, unspeakable things happen that don't make much sense, but God is not done with us yet. He uses the bending and the breaking and the dying to prepare the harvest, to prepare more for us. We reach high to the Son and He comes down and pulls us closer. We lift our heads to Him in awe and know that there might be hard around the corner but that we can look expectantly even to the bowing and the breaking, even the death of all we have planned, because we know in Him there will always be more. He sees the seeds that come with all the endings and is faithful to use them, to turn them into beauty.

I clung to the truth that there was beauty here and now in the waiting, not just in the outcome I was anticipating for Katherine, for her children, for our family. As I watched the sunflowers out the window, their faces lifted to the sun, I thought of Abraham, waiting all those years for his promised son. Again and again, God reminded me to have eyes like my children: eager and expectant.

We waited, but Katherine didn't get better. On New Year's Eve, friends and neighbors gathered around a bonfire in our backyard to watch fireworks. We roasted hot dogs and marshmallows, part of my ongoing efforts to preserve a sense of normalcy for my children in this unconventional life I had chosen for us. Grasping Katherine's hand and holding her youngest son in my lap on the couch, I listened through the open window as kids oohed and ahhed outside. At just four years old, John was her buddy and wasn't willing to leave her side to join the fun outside.

The next morning, she was noticeably worse and in a lot of pain. We took her to the hospital to explain to the doctor we had been working closely with that her agony was only increasing. I wonder if I would have done anything differently that day if I had known she wouldn't come back to our living room again. I wonder if I would have prepared my heart or her children or mine a little better. But I was believing for *healing,* waiting on it, expectant.

The doctor did a scan and gave us more news we didn't want to hear: Katherine's digestive tract had completely stopped moving, causing an obstruction, which was the source of her severe pain. Apart from surgery, there was nothing we could do, and Katherine was still too thin and weak to undergo anesthesia. I drove to the store to get some things for supper, then went home and, as if it were any ordinary night, rolled out pizza dough and asked the girls to help me grate cheese. Once we all had eaten, I drove my kids and hers to the hospital, where we sat and waited for more information from the doctors on what we could possibly do next.

Katherine spent six long agonizing nights in the hospital. I went home and back a lot, as the hospital was close by. Several friends took shifts with our children and household responsibilities. I sat with her in the hospital late into the night, sometimes into the early morning. Close friends came and sat with me and helped me sift through all that the doctors were saying and asked if there were any other options. I look back and marvel at how many people stepped in and loved us so that I could just keep loving her. In hindsight, I see it: they were God's provision, my ram in the thicket. At the time, all I could see was that Katherine needed to be loved. Whether she was healed or not, we would make sure that in this time she was well loved.

She couldn't eat, and a fluid IV drip in her arm seemed to be the only thing sustaining her life. Slowly she lost the ability to speak and only groaned, her periods of consciousness growing less and less frequent. I read again and again, out loud to her but also to myself, "O God, you are my God, earnestly I seek you; my soul thirsts for you, my body longs for you, in a dry and weary land where there is no water."[2] She was thirsty, her lips parched and cracking, and I was thirsty to see God here. We cried out to Him. But my desperate pleading and earnest seeking wouldn't yield the outcome I was looking for, not this time.

On the evening of our sixth day at the hospital, with a loud cry of agony, Katherine died.

8

YET I WILL
REJOICE

WHAT DO YOU DO WHEN you believe for life and ask for it with all
your heart, yet your friend still ends up dead and sealed up in a coffin?
What about when you go home from the hospital in the wee hours of the
morning and her children are asleep in your living room and you wonder
what you will tell them, what you will tell your own children who prayed
and believed with you? What do you do when God doesn't show up in
the way that you asked Him to? What was all that hoping for if this was
to be the end?

Relentless questions rolled through my mind. Ever the God wrestler,
I wanted to scream at Him for failing to come through. Truth be told, I
really just couldn't believe she was dead. Life with her family had become
normal life to us and it was jarring to go back to a "normal" that didn't
feel normal at all. Weeks passed and I couldn't believe that it had been so
many days since I had patted her sweet head and said good night to her

small frame on my couch. I couldn't believe that it wasn't just yesterday that I sat behind her in her hospital bed, holding her body in the only position that was comfortable for her in those final hours. As naive as it seems, I couldn't believe that it had ended this way after all our prayers, after all our hopes and dreams.

The silence in our home after Katherine's death threatened to choke us. Her children went to stay with a relative, and though our house was still relatively full, it felt empty. The silence screamed of failure, of prayers unanswered, of hope denied. We had waited, expectantly. We had believed that God would come through.

Despite the emptiness created by her absence, in the days surrounding Katherine's death, God felt nearer to me than He ever had before. And He whispered, *Come. Come to me all you who are weary.* So I did. I sat each night alone on the floor of my bathroom, the place that had become my little prayer closet in the last months when every other room in the house held sleeping people. I would come and I would sit and I would wait for Him. In the late-night hours alone with the Lord on the cold, hard floor, I beat my fists against the smooth tile and against my strong Father's chest, saying "How could You let her die?" and sobbing until words wouldn't come anymore.

I asked hard questions of God. I didn't understand how He could have allowed me to believe so strongly that Katherine would live when that wasn't His intent. How could a loving Father see me in my hope, know what I was believing for, and simultaneously know that the ending would *not* be the one I was hoping and believing for? It felt unfair, even cruel, and I let Him know it.

The Old Testament prophet Habakkuk also voiced His complaints to the Lord. A prophet in the time before Babylon conquered Jerusalem, Habakkuk was burdened by the violence and injustice that he witnessed all around him. He cried out, "How long, O Lord?" and "Why?"[1] He questioned God extensively, wondering why a good God would allow such iniquity to even exist, why He didn't come quickly to make things right. "Are You not hearing me, Lord?" he wondered. "Are You not listening?" Really, I think it is a question we are all asking, a question we must ask if we are truly to believe in and trust the unchanging character of a good, redemptive God in this world of hurt. When we look around and what we see does not match up with what we understand to be God's desire for full and joyous lives for His people, we are compelled to ask, "Lord, why do You allow such suffering?"

Though I didn't want to admit it, and maybe it took me months to articulate, I felt that maybe God had not heard our cries for help or, worse, maybe He had ignored them. I thrashed against Him and hurled these ugly accusations at Him, but still I could not deny the fact that He was near. His peace was evident in our home. His love wrapped around me like a warm embrace. He didn't take away my pain; He held me while I hurt.

Six weeks later, it was Katherine's little boy's sixth birthday. We had talked for weeks about the party we would have, with a cake, but that was when they still lived with us, when David's mother still lived. Instead, we drove across the bridge to where the children now lived with their aunt, who reluctantly was keeping them while we looked for other, more permanent options. We brought treats. We sang "Happy Birthday" and the kids played happily for several hours, thrilled to be reunited with their friends. I played with them too, pushing aside for a time the questions and the anger over their current situation. And as we drove away and we all smiled and waved to them out the van windows, I cried.

I didn't want the story to end this way.

I had written the ending in my head, one where my friend gets better, becomes strong and healthy, and is able to move out with her children. It was the ending where we would all cry happy tears as we served them their last meal before they headed out to their new life, healthy and whole. To me, *that* was the ending that would most glorify God. *That* was the one that would allow people to see Him clearly at work. In the ending I wrote, I didn't have to look into the eyes of four children under the age of ten as I bounced their baby sister on my knee to keep her quiet and tell them that their mother died in the night. In my ending, I didn't spend every hour of six consecutive days fighting for a mother to get well, only to end up clinging to my friend, Shana, as together we lowered a body into a casket.

I wonder if Habakkuk wrote different endings and different scenarios in his mind too, if he walked the ramparts of Jerusalem hoping and praying that Israel's story would take a different turn, that the violence and injustice in the city would miraculously halt, that God would intervene and stop allowing justice to be perverted.

God answers Habakkuk, though I wonder if His answer is really what Habakkuk is looking for. "Watch and wait," God says. "Look at the nations and watch—and be utterly amazed. For I am going to do something in your days that you would not believe."[2] It sounds hopeful, doesn't it? But God goes on to reveal that His plan for Israel's redemption involves catastrophic hurt and suffering first. He is going to raise up the Babylonians to conquer Judah, God's chosen people. If I had to guess, I'd say this probably isn't what Habakkuk had hoped for, not the ending he had anticipated.

Habakkuk asks the natural next questions, the questions I was grappling with, ones we all grapple with: "Why do it this way, God? Isn't there a better way?" Habakkuk knows the character of God, and because he knows God's goodness, he is troubled by the suffering God intends to allow. Wouldn't a different story glorify God more?

My favorite part of the story is Habakkuk's response. Rather than curl inward in anger and pity, as was my inclination, Habakkuk waits resolutely for God to show him His plans: "I will stand at my watch and station myself on the ramparts; I will look to see what he will say to me."[3] Faithful Habakkuk climbs up on his watchtower and waits for God. Habakkuk anticipates that God will indeed meet him there, and he is willing to wait.

I asked God repeatedly why He allowed me to believe so strongly that Katherine would live when she wasn't actually going to. Slowly He began to show me that He gave me the grace to believe that she would live so that in her final days she would feel hope and high spirits all around her, so that she would feel that she was fought for and that she was worth the fight.

Around the time of her death, many had consoled me with the statement "God is sovereign." While I knew this to be true, it felt like an insincere platitude. God being sovereign in this event simply meant to me that God had known and seen the ending yet still allowed me to persist in prayer and hope. Although I did not question God's sovereignty, it was not His absolute power or divine will that brought me comfort. One friend whispered a different statement in my ear, one that stuck with me throughout the months of grieving Katherine's death and even later that same year when faced with the possibility of further loss and grief.

"God is gracious," she said, and it rang true.

God was gracious in allowing my heart a true and undefiled hope for Katherine, for her children and mine. God was gracious in bringing her home to be with Him, free from the suffering and pain of this world. And He was gracious in holding us all near during that time. God is gracious always in providing His Son, our way to eternal life, our promise of life, fuller life, after death. And because I knew this, I could be certain that He would be gracious again.

God's answers came to me like this, unfolding slowly, gently. He was growing me and shaping me in my hope because my eager anticipation for Him had drawn me to His feet. In my hope and waiting, regardless of the outcome, I had known Him. And I would continue to know Him in this place. Night after night as I sought Him in the quiet after Katherine's death, I began to realize that my great hoping, my great expectancy, had grown in me both a hunger for God and an understanding of His love for us that I had not realized before. My belief that He would heal her had grown more room in my heart for Him. And now, in this emptiness, He was all that would fill it.

When I had nowhere to turn, He was the only place I could come home to.

Like Habakkuk, I desired simply a reprieve from suffering. We had watched Katherine die, and now we watched her children struggle in the home of a relative who didn't really desire to care for them. Their aunt was young and had no experience raising children. Unemployed, she was unable to cope with the added burden of five mouths to feed, even with our help. Understandably, she too was grieving the unexpected loss of her older sister. It broke my heart to see the children so seemingly neglected, often going to bed hungry after another relative yet again sold off the food we brought. Months later, they continued wearing the same clothes we had taken them home in, which were now filthy. They felt scared and unwelcome in this place without their mother to fend for them. We were devastated for them.

Habakkuk asks God when He will end the suffering of the Israelites, and God answers that first He will raise up the Babylonians to conquer them. I resonate with Habakkuk as he protests the Lord's answer. More suffering? Now? But why?

Our own family also was feeling the deep pain of loss. Sometimes I would find one of my daughters in her room in tears, unable to fully put words to her hurt. Not only were we all broken over Katherine's death, but my children also missed their friends tremendously. We often made the drive over the bridge to pick them up for afternoon playdates and the occasional sleepover. We always picked them up for church on Sunday morning, bringing their aunt when she would agree to come.

Many of my children, having experienced the loss of their own biological parents, seemed to grieve all over again alongside their friends. This loss dug up past hurt that some of them were still processing. My sadness was more about Katherine's kids' current situation. Although they were still attending school, they were clearly not being cared for very attentively by their remaining relatives. A kind neighbor came to me and expressed concern that on the days she did not feed them, she was uncertain of whether they received a meal. We provided more food and all the support we could to the extended family, but they continued to make clear that we should look for another solution for the children. Despite my growing awareness of God's presence, my questions remained, and new ones continued to surface as I witnessed the hurt of my children and the suffering of Katherine's, all of which I was powerless to stop.

At night I often sat alone with my Father and wept for the suffering that I could not understand or explain or fix. I asked like Habakkuk, *Why this way, God? Why would You allow it? Isn't there a better way to show the world Your glory?* In response to my questions, God continued to assure me in the dark, quiet evenings that my hope was not in vain and that my watching and waiting was growing my capacity for Him.

While researching for a Bible study on something else, I stumbled across an explanation that Habakkuk's name is derived from the Hebrew word for "to embrace" and that the name *Habakkuk* literally means "he who clings." Yes. These days full of things that I could not explain or fix were not just my invitation to wait and watch but my great instruction to *cling* to the only One who remains constant in all our circumstances, in both joy and sorrow.

Habakkuk is devastated by the destruction he witnesses; he watches it all unfold almost helplessly. Yet by the end of the short book, this is his prayer:

> Though the fig tree does not bud
>   and there are no grapes on the vines,
> though the olive crop fails
>   and the fields produce no food,
> though there are no sheep in the pen
>   and no cattle in the stalls,
> yet I will rejoice in the LORD,
>   I will be joyful in God my Savior.
>
> The Sovereign LORD is my strength;
>   he makes my feet like the feet of a deer,
>   he enables me to go on the heights.[4]

When we cannot find joy in our circumstances, we can find joy in God, who is unchanged and unchanging. We can rejoice not in what is going on around or within us but because He is our strength and will continue to be.

We look at pain and wonder why God would allow it. Sometimes the fig tree does not bud and there are no sheep in the pen. Sometimes the olive trees look bare and the stalls look empty and the world looks bleak. Sometimes we are climbing Mount Moriah, unsure of what God is doing or why He asks this of us. But even as we wonder why, even as we wait, we are the ones who *cling* to the Lord. We can say with Habakkuk that we will rejoice—not because we enjoy the barrenness and the brokenness, but because God will be our strength. Even in the midst of seemingly impossible circumstances, we can experience His presence and can trust in His ultimate goodness. Our pain can bring about an intimacy with God that we otherwise might not know.

In grief and uncertainty, I knew a God who was both good and personal. A God who *loved me.*

Slowly but surely, He was teaching me that death is not the end. The end was when He rose from a tomb. I had asked for life, and Life is what He gave. Better, glorious, eternal Life. In those final hours, I held my friend's head and watched her breath leave her body as her soul first laid eyes on His face, and I could nearly feel His breath on mine. I do not know His ways, but I know Him. *I know Him.* And I do not lay my friends before Jesus for just physical healing but that they might know Him too, that they might be saved.

A watching world might say, "Why hope for life in a world of death?" And we know the answer. This world is not all there is, and death is not the end. Our fight is not for this life. Our fight is for eternity. And a hope for eternity truly cannot disappoint.

In the dark season, He doesn't leave. In fact, He draws near. He whispers that loving people is not in vain because in loving people, we know more of Him, regardless of the end result. God is love, and as we love in His name, He is glorified. And this is where I find hope: in knowing that He will be glorified.

9

SCARS

"COME, ALL YOU WHO are thirsty, come to the waters; and you who have no money, come, buy and eat!"[1] Children circled the table for breakfast and scarfed down bananas and spread peanut butter on bread as I read Isaiah 55 for our morning devotions. I had picked it haphazardly, and unbeknownst to them, it was like a promise straight from God to my soul.

"Come, buy wine and milk without money and without cost. Why spend money on what is not bread, and your labor on what does not satisfy? Listen, listen to me, and eat what is good, and your soul will delight in the richest of fare. Give ear and come to me; hear me, *that your soul may live.*"[2]

Six months after Katherine had gone to be with Jesus, after six months of watching her children struggle as relatives bounced them from one home to another, no one quite ready to take on this brood, today was the day we would move them in with their permanent foster family. I wanted so badly to be filled with excitement about this day, had even anticipated the joy I would feel, and as I sat here now I did feel those things, but the loss still felt so close.

And then in this passage from Isaiah, God assured me that He saw all the questions and fears and was answering.

> You will go out in joy
>   and be led forth in peace;
> the mountains and hills
>   will burst into song before you,
> and all the trees of the field
>   will clap their hands.
> Instead of the thornbush will grow the pine tree,
>   and instead of briers the myrtle will grow.
> This will be for the LORD's renown,
>   for an everlasting sign,
>   which will not be destroyed.[3]

This passage was such a stark contrast to the prayer I had yelled out just hours before Katherine's death: "My soul thirsts for you . . . in a dry and weary land where there is no water."[4] His answer to me, the answer He had been whispering to me and teaching me for the last half of a year as I grappled with grief and questions, was, *Come to Me, thirsty one. Come to Me, and you will not be thirsty anymore.* Continually, He offered a gentle reminder that His ways were not my ways and that all that now seemed desolate, like a thornbush, would one day spring up in new life for His own renown.

It's a strange thing, unnatural really, to look out at the brier patch and hope for flowers, to see life's thornbushes and wait for the growth of a lush pine tree instead, to name the mountain The Lord Will Provide when you are surrounded by a dense, bare-branched thicket. It seems almost foolish to look at the wasteland and close your eyes and believe for streams and fertility and abundance. Yet this was His call to me, to us, again and again. *Look for Me here. Expect Me here. Push aside those thoughts that say "What if He doesn't show up?" and just expect that I will.*

Moving the children to their foster home today would be joyous, but it would be hard. Could I look wide-eyed in wonder at Jesus and keep expecting the promise of His redemption, this beauty from ashes, these streams in the desert, a shoot from the stump? Could I believe that He might truly have a good ending here after all, that these dear children would have a stable and loving home at last?

The road to this day had been long and achingly hard. After many months of observing, I saw that Katherine's children were not thriving under the care of their extended family members. We had given all the support we could, but even the family agreed that it was not working. They had so many challenges of their own and did not have the capacity to give five small children the energy, attention, and provision they required. I had spent hours asking God to show me how to best help them and give me wisdom for doing so with grace and sensitivity.

On a Tuesday morning, I shared with a friend my devastating realization that I just didn't know how to make sure Katherine's children were taken care of; it seemed we had exhausted all our options. That very same afternoon, I went to visit our friend Rose to talk about something different entirely. However, it wasn't lost on me what a phenomenal mother she was and the fact that her youngest would be leaving for boarding school in just one more year. In the back of my mind, I wondered if she would be a good candidate for becoming a foster mom, but I knew I could never ask this of someone. She and I prayed together and

I began to speak, but not halfway through my first sentence, she interrupted me.

"Before we talk about that," she began, "I just have to ask you about those children who used to stay with you, the ones who lost their mother." I listened, surprised. "God just keeps putting them on my heart. I'm sure you have them well taken care of and they are fine, but I just feel that I wouldn't be obeying the Spirit if I didn't ask you if they need anything. If there is anything I can do? If even, maybe, they need someplace to go?"

I didn't know whether to laugh or cry. The memory verse I had recited with my children that morning during homeschool rang through my ears, their little voices shouting with excitement: "We rejoice in the hope of the glory of God. . . . And hope *does not disappoint us,* because God has poured out his love into our hearts by the Holy Spirit, whom he has given us."[5] Without a doubt, the Spirit had come before me and prepared Rose's heart for something that was much bigger than anything I could dream up.

Her eyes glistened as I explained the situation the children were in. Rose had been a short-term foster parent before but recently had been praying about becoming a long-term one, specifically for these children, whom she'd observed when we brought them with us to church. Convinced that God had provided her as the answer to my prayers, we made plans to speak with the family later that day. When we explained to them Rose's offer, the aunts and uncles felt as blessed as I had at the thought of these children having a permanent and stable home with a strong and loving mother just around the corner from their biological family, who would be able to see them often. We began pursuing the paperwork necessary to make this happen.

Meanwhile, I invited Rose to join us for dinner the following Sunday so we could officially introduce Katherine's children to their new foster family. It was only later that I realized that Sunday would be Mother's Day, which seemed like extra confirmation from God, a wink and a nod to say, *I am in this.*

On Sunday my girls and I excitedly chopped vegetables and prepared chicken and rice to get ready for our dinner guests. Katherine's children arrived without any idea what significance this day held for all of us and excitedly ran to the backyard to play with their friends. Later, Rose and her two daughters arrived, looking around expectantly. I could hardly contain all my emotions of the moment. The whole day long, my children had graciously celebrated me as their mother. Now I grieved the loss of a mother for these children and yet looked, full of joy and hope, on the kind and gentle face of the woman who would step into this role.

We introduced the children to her, and they crowded around her on the couch. The two little boys were quick to smile and run back to play, but the girls, a little bit older and grasping more clearly what this meant, did not leave Rose's side for the rest of the evening. Together we cooked, shared a meal, and did dishes. Later, as Rose and I sat on the couch chatting about the future, all our children—mine, hers, Katherine's—danced and sang loudly in a circle on the front porch.

I peered out the window at them and was overwhelmed at the joy God had given and continued to give, the resilience of these little hearts laughing and playing together. My fierce prayer was that they would always remember the joy He had given us in this place. The words I had read in my devotional earlier that morning rang through my mind as I watched them double over in laughter:

The difference between shallow happiness and a deep, sustaining joy is sorrow. Happiness lives where sorrow is not. When sorrow arrives, happiness dies. It can't stand pain. Joy, on the other hand, rises from sorrow and therefore can withstand all grief. Joy, by the grace of God, is the transfiguration of suffering into endurance, and of endurance into character, and of character into hope—and the hope that has become our joy does not (as happiness must for those who depend upon it) disappoint us.[6]

There had been trials and pain, so many imperfect days. There had been deep sorrow. But up out of our sorrow, God brought joy. Hope in Him had become our sustaining joy—joy that could never disappoint us.

Several weeks later, just hours after I read God's assurances in Isaiah 55, we moved the children into their new home. Their foster mama came with us as we went back and forth from their old house to hers. She grinned from ear to ear as we piled all their things into our already-crowded van.

"I am excited, Rose!" I had said.

"Oh, I am more excited!" she had proclaimed as the kids bounced and laughed in the back seats, and we had smiled, happy.

But as I stepped out of the van into this new yard and looked at the new house they would live in and this new family, my heart felt the very obvious hole: we were missing someone. Katherine wasn't here. What was happening was good, and beautiful even, but it was not as I had imagined a year ago, not as I had hoped.

Their future flashed before me, and I imagined them growing and laughing and learning and playing in this place. And I wanted their mom. I wanted their mom standing there in the yard with me to see how happy her children were and how good God had made it. I desired desperately to acknowledge the redemption of a new family in this new place, but I wanted their mom to watch them grow and laugh and learn and play in this place too. And though I tried, I couldn't stop the tears that streamed down my face.

Rose came up behind me and wrapped her strong arms around my shoulder, as if she had silently understood my thoughts. I could hardly whisper, "Thank you. Oh, thank you for being willing to welcome and love them like this."

"God is faithful," she replied simply, and she cried with me. She cried with me and for them and their loss, and God confirmed it all in my heart again: this was His best for them right now. He was making all things new, even beauty out of this brokenness.

I prayed Isaiah 55 aloud as we knelt on the cement floor of their home. There we gathered: my five little friends who had lost their mother six months ago, even though it felt like just yesterday; their new foster mother, willing and ready; my children who had witnessed all of it with me; and me. Their eighteen-year-old sister came too, the one who had helped me care for her mother in those final days. She had just given birth to a new baby boy who had her late mother's chin, and she had named him Emmanuel, "God is with us," because He is. God's promise from Isaiah was perfect for this day—that when we come thirsty, He satisfies, and that when come looking for Him, we find Him.

I still wondered why He would let it happen this way, but I had learned to listen for His whisper. *I didn't change My mind in My love for them,* He spoke. *I didn't change My mind in My love for them or for you. I love you, I go before you, and I never fail. I never fail.*

He said, *Come thirsty. Eat what is good. I alone will satisfy. Come broken. Come empty. Come wounded. And instead of a thornbush, I will grow a pine tree. You will go out in joy and be led forth in peace, and I will make it beautiful for My own renown alone, for My glory, so the world might know Me.*

Oh, Lord, may it be.

So my girls mopped their house and we made their beds with new sheets, clean and crisp. We helped them settle in, and I didn't stop praying. One at a time, I held their little faces in my hands. "I love you, you know?" They nod. "And God loves you. He knows you miss your mom, and that is okay with Him. He knows your pain, and He hasn't forgotten it or ignored it. He loves you so much that He wants to give you something new, but it doesn't mean you have to forget the old. He wants to grow something beautiful out of your pain." They are little. They nod and giggle and run off to play with their friends.

Except David. He sits in my lap for a long time. He is angry. I remember how he responded two weeks ago when I told him he was going to have a foster mom, my voice cheerful. His six-year-old eyes looked back into mine and he said, "I don't want a new mom. I want my old mom." And I held him and whispered into his ear, "Me too, buddy. Me too. I wanted it differently too. It will be okay. It will be okay." Today I hold him once more and say it over and over and over again in his ear while I ask it silently to the Lord: *It will be okay, right?*

And my strong Father holds me while I flail. He sees my mess of joy and pain and peace and doubt and sadness all jumbled together and cradles it all in His strong Father arms. I have to believe that He cradles these children too. I know He does.

And one day He will come. We will look upon His face and He will wipe away every tear and all our mourning and sadness, and death will be no more, and we will worship Him forever. *Glory.*

Everyone is done unpacking. We get back in the van, and my kids are still basking in their excitement over what they have been able to do for their friends. "Rise and shine and give God the glory, glory. Rise and shine . . . ," sings the littlest. Yes, for all He is doing and all He has yet to do, we give Him all the glory for joy in this place.

Later that evening, I sat for a while near the fire that we had cooked our hot dogs over and listened to the laughter of children chasing after lightning bugs in the dark. I had begged God to open my eyes to the beauty all around me as I watched Katherine's children move into their new home with their new family. They had smiled and they had her smile. I wanted to praise God, to recognize His goodness in bringing redemption and a new family and a new home, but I still felt that deep sting of loss.

I sat on a stump near the bonfire with Mack, the stranger-turned-friend-turned-family who had just silently lived it all with us, this season of hard and hurt. We both stared long at the fire dancing, and then he turned to me. It has been years since I thought of him as someone we were helping. Now he is just a part of us. But as he turned to me, I noticed that he was looking at the scar on his leg. He gestured toward it. That scar, that wound that I had scraped and cleaned and bandaged, that wound that had healed me as much as it had healed him. I looked at it and I gasped. I had completely forgotten how big it was. He had been so fine and so happy and healed for so long now that I had forgotten how large and deep the wound really was, how it stretched from his knee to his ankle, wrapping around his calf, and how it was so deep that we could touch the bone. It seemed like so long ago.

Mack's eye caught mine and he smiled. "I will wear this scar with me," he said. "I will wear it wherever I go. And I will think of you. I will always, always think of you and remember that God was so faithful to me and that you were faithful too." He is moving out soon. He is ready to go. He has a steady job and a love for Jesus that could take him anywhere, and he doesn't know just how much he will be missed or just how much his words mean to me.

I told him of how we spent the day moving Katherine's children into their new foster home, and I smiled through the tears. He listened, nodding with a deep understanding of God, who is so good in our pain. We all have scars. My heart scars were readily on display here in the glow of the fire.

We all have scars, and by them we remember the hard times we've endured. So much hard and so much pain. But God healed us! He was good to *us*. He grew new cells and new skin and new life out of the hard, wounded places, and one day we look back at the scar and we gasp. We think of how deep and vast our pain was, and we can hardly believe what God has made it.

I have known this redemption to be true, and it gives me hope that it will be true again. I ask the Lord for the heart of Mack. May we carry our scars not as burdens but as constant reminders of His faithfulness and goodness to us. May we look at the healed places and say, "Wherever I go, I will always remember His faithfulness here."

I miss my friend. I am sad for her children, and I am sad that she was not there today to see their sweet smiles and excitement or to hold David and tell him that it would be okay. I want to sit with her just one last time and tell her that we took care of them. I want to tell her that we found them the very best family we could and that we tried hard to love them well. I want her to know.

But I know that she is busy gazing at His face, worshipping before the throne of the Creator. And I hear Him whisper to me, *I see you. I see you trying and I see you loving them, and I see you providing them with the very best you can. I will heal this place for each of you, and I will make it a place of My new life and glory. You, and they, will carry these scars with heads high to tell of My goodness to you.*

God has not changed His mind about His love for me or His love for them. He sees our pain. He knows the depth and breadth, and He chooses to love us through it and out of it. He chooses to grow beauty here not just to move us beyond our pain but to use it to shape us into His likeness.

The scars whisper of His glory. The scars mean that we are growing, and the biggest scars prove His faithfulness all the more.

Children dance in the firelight, and their laughter echoes loud in the dark. I can't help but think of all He has done here—the beauty He has made from nothing. I see His glory. I know His kindness, always calling us home.

10

COME TO LIFE

BEFORE I KNEW IT, the rainy season had come and gone and again our backyard was a blanket of sunflowers. Seven months had flown by, months when I felt I accomplished very little other than to simply sit with Jesus and, by His grace, keep my household running.

As I slowly began to come up for air, I realized that the long season of struggling through grief had changed me, grown me in my affection for God and a realization of my undeniable need for Him. It had also forced me to take a step back in ministry. Although I continued mothering my baker's dozen and welcoming people in need into our home, I had drastically decreased my day-to-day involvement in Amazima and any ministry outside our home. Some days this felt so right; other days it felt unproductive, as if I wasn't doing enough or being enough if I couldn't point to tangible results and accomplishments. I read the most beautiful quote in the book *Sensing Jesus,* by Zack Eswine:

> God will give you a place to inhabit, which means that you get to become attentive to what is there where you are. This means that

to dwell knowledgeably and hospitably in and toward the place
God gives you is to glorify him. God will give you a few things
that he intends for you to do in your inhabited place and with
those people. To do what God gives you to do is to strengthen
the common good and to glorify him.[1]

This is such a simple truth, yet it strikes my heart in a profound way.
To dwell in the place I have been given. To do the things I have been
given. To love the people I have been given. This is not mysterious or far
reaching, yet this is the truth of a God-ordained life.

Slowly, I was beginning to understand that it wasn't my productivity
that God desired; it was my heart. It wasn't my ministry God loved; it
was me. God was glorified, *is glorified,* when we give Him our hearts,
give Him ourselves, and faithfully do the thing right in front of us, no
matter how small or trivial.

Maybe this took me a while to grasp because early on in my adult
life, God gave me some pretty extraordinary things to do. I had a large
family, and I directed a large and growing-larger ministry, leading a huge
team to serve more than a thousand families. These endeavors were easy
to write stories about, and as I looked at the results, it was easy to believe
that He was using me as He accomplished extraordinary things in,
through, and all around me.

By contrast, in these recent months, God had been teaching me the
extraordinary strength it takes to just be ordinary. To dwell knowledgeably and hospitably in and toward this place He has given me with my
people is, in fact, an extraordinary call. He has shown me the beauty of
being attentive to one person, in the mundane, again and again: to sit
and listen to a mother's frustration over her child, to notice a downcast
teenager's face and ask about her day at school, to sit and play Candy
Land for what feels like the millionth time, to joyfully receive a gift I

don't need from a neighbor who desires to bless, to love people so much that I take great pleasure in not words or programs or projects but my very life with them.

In a full life of trying to do great big things for God and see His glory in great big ways, He showed me that He is glorified in the small too. He is glorified in each pot of pasta faithfully put on the table for our people. He is glorified each time we look into a stranger's eyes and acknowledge the person's humanity. He is glorified when we turn to focus on Him instead of focusing on our lack, and He is glorified when we help our child with her hundredth math problem even though we have already explained repeatedly the steps to a solution. Our God is not too big for the small and is glorified in our ordinary moments as we invite Him in. When I invite Him into my tiny and ordinary, even mundane moments become extraordinary. Small acts of love become whispers of His glory in the midst of our everydayness.

I believe without a doubt that God poured out His blessing on my early years of ministry, when fast growth seemed unstoppable and the easy-to-write stories with their miraculous endings were many. But over time, He has been showing me an even deeper truth: that when all those things pass away, He will remain. When the ministry feels stagnant and there is no astonishing growth to show for long hours of hard work, on days I don't receive extraordinary answers to prayer, He is still glorified in my faithful pursuit of Him.

During this season when most of my ministry had taken place inside the walls of my home and the most growth had taken place inside my own heart, I felt hidden away in Him. When no one else saw how I wrestled with grief, when no one saw how I struggled with the same child again and again, when no one saw all the noses wiped and laundry folded and toilets scrubbed, God was being glorified.

I was learning that, ultimately, our hidden reach for God counts so much more than our public one. Some people might look at my life and say how amazing I am or what a radical Christian I am, just as some people might praise you because you appear to have it all together, but what really counts will be the quiet devotion practiced in our own homes. What will matter most at the end of our lives are these people right in front of us who get to see all of it, the happy stories and the tragic ones, the pretty-good parts of us and the ugliest parts of us. At the end of time, all that will count is that we lived the Gospel with our very lives, that we paid attention to the people God gave us and dwelt knowledgeably and hospitably in the place to which He called us.

I think often on the miracles of Jesus. He did a lot of healing. And although the physical healing of ailments and casting out of demons certainly brought God glory and demonstrated to those watching His unsurpassable power, I suspect the physical healing was often beside the point. All the people Jesus healed would later become sick again. Those He fed with the loaves and fish would be hungry in a matter of hours. Even Jairus's daughter and Lazarus himself, raised from the dead, would one day die again. Maybe the point of all these miracles isn't just the healing, or isn't the healing at all, but the great compassion with which Jesus turns toward people.

I am struck by the way He stops what He is doing to look at one person, no matter how "terrible" the person might be, how different the person might be, how unclean or sinful the person might be. Jesus stops what He is doing, He looks at these people, and He sees them. And the God of all mercy and comfort is *moved* to compassion for His people. He is moved to compassion for the crowd, and He is moved to compassion for the one.

Again and again, He stops. He sees His people. He looks into their eyes and acknowledges their pain and acknowledges their sin, and He is not repulsed. He does not turn away. Jesus looks at them and loves them. He holds their hands. He takes the nails in His own hands for their sin. He promises that one day there will be no tears because He will wipe them all away.

Dear one, the Savior of the world does the same for you and for me. He looks at us and really sees us. He sees our sin and our mess and our pain and does not turn away.

I think that as humans, each of us just as lacking as the next, the most powerful thing we can do for another person is not to try to fix his or her pain or make it go away but to acknowledge it. I cannot heal. I cannot perform miracles. Even for all my trying, I cannot make sure that someone will receive salvation from Jesus. But I can be a witness. I can look at another's broken, bleeding mess and say, "I see you. I am with you. I will not turn away."

It is a great honor to share the life of another, to bear witness in a way that says, "You matter. This matters. Your story matters." Because it does. It matters to God.

During my time of quiet ministry in my own home, God brought many others into our lives who needed someone to sit with them in their hurt, acknowledge them, and love them in their pain. We live just down the road from the main hospital, an easily accessible place for patients in need of good medical care from the hospital and the comfort and nurture of a family home. It seemed only right that we should open our home to those in need. As I think back, I find it remarkable to remember all the people who filled our lives during that season, and the girls and I fondly recount story after story of those He brought to our home.

A young, scared mother came with her sweet baby, just two months old, who had a terminal skin condition that caused burn-like blisters to cover his body. Ultimately, infection from these wounds would lead to his death. She stayed with us while doctors ran countless tests on her son, and even after they moved out, she came to visit several times a week just to pray and be encouraged. A grandfather from our community whom we had just recently established a relationship with was diagnosed with cancer, everywhere, and given a few weeks to live. And then there was Betty, who looked a lot like Katherine and whose illness was so similar to Katherine's—Betty, whom I was afraid to love, because I was afraid she would die.

We opened our home and our hearts wide and served these people. We talked with them and listened to them, served them dinner and prayed with them, drove them to hospital visits and assured them that God was with them, even when their situations might indicate otherwise.

As I thought on the seeming hopelessness of their circumstances, God brought to mind the story of the prophet Ezekiel and the valley of dry bones. God led him to a valley of skeletons and asked him if the bones could live.

> The hand of the LORD was upon me, and he brought me out by the Spirit of the LORD and set me in the middle of a valley; it was full of bones. He led me back and forth among them, and I saw a great many bones on the floor of the valley, bones that were very dry. He asked me, "Son of man, can these bones live?"
>
> I said, "O Sovereign LORD, you alone know."
>
> Then he said to me, "Prophesy to these bones and say to them, 'Dry bones, hear the word of the LORD! This is what the Sovereign LORD says to these bones: I will make breath enter you, and you will come to life. I will attach tendons to you and make flesh come upon you and cover you with skin; I will put breath in you, and you will come to life. Then you will know that I am the LORD.' "[2]

I had read this story before, encouraged by the obvious promise that God would look at the people of Israel, at all of us sinners, and speak new life into them, into us. This time, though, I read it in a new light. So many of these people who were coming to live with us looked, on the outside, like these hopeless dry bones. Their situations were dire and their futures seemed grim.

Maybe we were the Ezekiels, those He had asked to speak new life into the dead and dry places, to prophesy over these people He brought us so that they, too, might know new life in Him. In bearing witness to their stories—in saying to them, "We see you and we are with you and we are for you"—we might be the vehicles God used to breathe life into weary, dry souls. And maybe we had been allowed to feel hopelessness and doubt so that we could speak life into those He brought us who were experiencing the same things for themselves. We, as witnesses both to their stories and to the story of the Gospel, could speak His life over them.

During this time, a gentleman named Joseph was sent to me by a doctor who had worked closely with us to treat Mack's wound. Joseph had a similar burn on his leg, and the doctor asked if I would help, as Mack's leg had healed so well.

I remember sitting with Joseph on the porch as I wrapped up his burn one day. "Aren't you afraid?" he asked.

"I was once." I smiled. "Taking care of wounds used to make my stomach churn. It was as if I could feel the pain just by looking at the wound, and even the thought of such pain was overwhelming."

"But now?" he asked, perplexed.

I looked down at the wound I had been bandaging for a few weeks and saw the signs of new pink life appearing at the edges.

"Well, now I really like to clean and bandage wounds, Joseph." I paused, trying to decide if it was even really possible to explain to him why. I thought of Mack's wound and all the healing that God had brought about in my own heart during that time, the way God still used his scar to remind me on days when life felt too hard and the pain too deep.

"Under all this dead skin on your leg, deep under the charred and burned part," I began to explain, "there is new life. We have to clean out all the dead, and when we do, God will miraculously grow new cells and new skin until we can hardly see the wound anymore. Do you see that pink part? He's already started. And the best part? I'm not even doing that much. I'm really just a spectator. I can't create skin. I can't give life. But I can be faithful. I can dress this wound every day, and I can watch God give life to the dead places."

He nodded, but I wasn't sure he was following.

"It's like my heart, Joseph." I took a breath and plunged on. "I come to God broken. I come with just a weak, feeble longing for the Lord, and He sees my wounds. He sees all the dead and barren places in my heart, the places where I am hurting, and He breathes life. Like with this new skin, He makes my heart new. He grows life in the dead places."

"So you're not afraid of wounds anymore?" Joseph laughed.

"No, I don't think I am. The pain can still be overwhelming sometimes, but I know that God is faithful. The deeper the wound and the bigger the pain, the more healing that can take place. Listen to this." I pulled out my Bible and began to read from Ezekiel the story that God had placed on my heart. "Can you imagine? Ezekiel is ankle deep in skeletons, and he just watches them come to life—stand up and *breathe*. I've never seen anything like this, Joseph, but I think God has done something like this in my heart. When I am sad and bitter and doubtful, He reminds me of who He is and breathes new life and new hope into me. And when I was dead in my sin and transgression, He sent His Son Jesus to die so that I wouldn't have to."

By this point, I was long done bandaging his leg and we were just sitting. His bandage that had showed up soaked with puss and filth had been replaced with one that was clean and crisp and white. I knew that it would be dirty again the next day, but I rejoiced in just a moment of pure white.

"It's like me. I come dirty—filthy in my sin and dead in my transgression. And He washes me white. He says that my sins are forgiven because of His Son, that my stains are wiped clean. I will mess up again and again, I'll come back dirty and battered, but His mercies will be new. And He will remind me again—again and again and again—that He shed His blood to wash my sin away, to make my heart clean and crisp and white, just like this bandage. Alive again, just like those dry bones.

"And one day, Joseph, we will stand before Him. We will stand before Him battered and bruised and wounded and filthy. We will stand before Him as those who spent their lives trying but still making mistakes, those who quickly shifted their eyes, those who brought just a weak, feeble obedience, and He will call us faithful because of His Son. He will call us to new life. We will wear white, like this bandage. And we will worship."

He laughed at me. "I guess you love wounds."

I laughed along with him, but to myself I thought, *No, I don't.* No one loves wounds. No one loves to stand in the valley of skeletons. But when we love our Savior, we can trust that sometimes the ugliness of life draws us to Him. No one loves to witness the depth of pain and suffering the world has to offer, but I do love to bear witness to the stories of those He brings into our lives. I love to speak of His faithfulness. Because He was faithful to me in my pain, in my wrestling, in my doubt, I can assure you He will be faithful to you in yours.

You, my people, will know that I am the LORD, when I open your graves and bring you up from them. I will put my Spirit in you and you will live, and I will settle you in your own land. Then you will know that I the LORD have spoken, and I have done it, declares the LORD.[3]

He says it to the Israelites, and He says it to me.

I saw this in my own home. The world might once have called my children or their early circumstances broken. As a young single mother with not much of a clue as to how to parent, I might have been labeled "broken" too. We probably looked like little more than a valley of dry bones sometimes. But God had called me and given me the great privilege of speaking life, of breathing His Word into their hurting places, of believing for them and with them that He had great purpose for them, not just one day but now. And faithfully He had brought such life into our home, on display most clearly as we cared for the people He brought us.

As I snuggled next to Scovia on the couch to read aloud, as I gave Sumini and Joyce my full attention while teaching them to frost cupcakes, I was breathing life into their little hearts, and God was using them to breathe life into mine. When I rejoiced with Grace over an accomplishment or new skill that she had been tirelessly working on in physical therapy, we celebrated this new life He was bringing forth.

As I helped Sarah with the many animals she rescued—puppies, hedgehogs, and Bo, the cat with only two legs—as I played Scrabble with Hellen in the kitchen while I cooked dinner, and as I kicked a soccer ball around the yard with Tibita despite my utter lack of skill, bones were coming together. We were being strengthened in God's love. Just as He had promised to the people of Israel through Ezekiel, He was taking all our once-dead places and giving them life.

He breathed life into us so that we could breathe it into others. He was good to us so that we could testify of His goodness. Our dry bones lived and called out to others that they, too, could have full and abundant life in Him.

11

Choosing
to Believe

She reaches for my hand and smiles. I reach for hers and force myself to return her smile, force myself to try to look truly joyful. I want her to know joy here. *I want to know joy here.*

At twenty-six years old, Betty is the beautiful mother of a three-year-old boy. She came to live with us a few months ago, one of the many people God brought to fill the gaping hole left after Katherine's death. She now weighs sixty-nine pounds and battles AIDS, tuberculosis, and all the complications that come with the two. This is beginning to feel all too familiar. The hand she reaches out reminds me so much of a hand I held so recently, of a woman I loved hard, of a friend who became a family member. As I look at Betty, I am afraid. Can we do this again? The question that I don't want to think reverberates in my head and I try to push it back: *What if You don't heal her, God? What if we get to know her, come to love her, and You take her too? I don't think I can do that again.*

I fight the tears and force a smile. After all, she might get better. She might live. And right now, I know she needs me to believe that she can live so that she can believe that she can.

How do you keep believing that when the last time you were wrong? When the time before that and the time before that you were wrong? I sit down on the side of my couch that is now her bed and ask her about her family. Even as we talk, I feel my heart start to put up a wall. *How invested should I get?* my flesh questions. I know better than to let my doubt get the best of me like this. I *should* know better, anyway. Haven't we repeatedly seen God's redemption in the hard?

Intellectually, I know that my job is to believe in His goodness without wavering. His job is *everything else.* But my heart can be so slow to remember. This is the sin of the Israelites, of all humankind really, this slowness to remember all that He has done as we stare intently at what He hasn't done yet, what He might not do. His answer is steady and true: *What if I don't, child? What if I don't heal her? What if My plan is different? Still I am with you. Still I am God.* I study her face, this woman, in her midtwenties just like me, a mother just like me. Life has dealt her a different hand, but her brown eyes are searching, just like mine. Her smile is gentle, genuine. God brings to mind a favorite miracle.

A large crowd followed and pressed around him. And a woman was there who had been subject to bleeding for twelve years. She had suffered a great deal under the care of many doctors and had spent all she had, yet instead of getting better she grew worse. When she heard about Jesus, she came up behind him in the crowd and touched his cloak, because she thought, "If I just touch his clothes, I will be healed." Immediately her bleeding stopped and she felt in her body that she was freed from her suffering. At once Jesus realized that power had gone out from him.

He turned around in the crowd and asked, "Who touched my clothes?"

"You see the people crowding against you," his disciples answered, "and yet you can ask, 'Who touched me?'"

But Jesus kept looking around to see who had done it. Then the woman, knowing what had happened to her, came and fell at his feet and, trembling with fear, told him the whole truth. He said to her, "Daughter, your faith has healed you. Go in peace and be freed from your suffering."[1]

I resonate deeply with this woman. I can see her pushing through the crowd, reaching out for Jesus's hem. I can feel the strain, that desperate reaching, longing to touch Him, just even the very edge of His robe. A longing for only Him. I imagine her inner pleading after trying so long to be healed: *Please, please.*

And I am like the woman with the issue of blood, except I am the woman with the issue of doubt. I am the woman with the issue of sin, with the issue of flesh, with the issue of forgetfulness. I am a woman who wants to snap my arms shut and protect, fold my arms tight around my chest to guard my heart, which is still so raw and exposed, protect it from being broken yet again. I want to gather my children to myself and shelter them from the ugly hurt of this world. My mind wanders too quickly from *He can* to *I can't,* and my focus turns to earthly struggles before it rests in my heavenly Father.

Like the woman with an issue of blood, I am desperately in need of His touch. According to Mosaic Law, this woman wasn't even allowed to be in the same room as Jesus, let alone touch Him. Her disease made her unclean, prohibited from mingling with the general public. To be discovered would have meant possible punishment and certain humiliation. Despicable. Dirty. Disgusting.

Toward this woman, *Jesus turns.* He sees her.

I can imagine His tenderness as He turns toward her. I can imagine His voice dispelling all her trembling fear and assuring her that reaching for Him was, in fact, the right and faithful thing to do. I imagine Him gently locking eyes with her, knowing her, loving her. I can imagine this because it is what He has done for me time and time again. I stretch out my shaky hand and He turns toward me, He sees me, He knows me.

I know deep in my Spirit that I want Jesus in the same way she did. But the truth is, I can't fold my arms to the hurt of this world and simultaneously reach out for my Savior. To reach for Him, I have no choice but to fling my arms wide again. I push aside the thoughts of hopelessness that cloud my mind and seek His compassion for the woman in front of me now, this woman so like me. *Give me Your eyes for her,* I pray. I reach for Betty's hand and I know, just like the bleeding woman, I must seek Jesus. *If only I touch His cloak . . .*

Hope is the great expectancy of this woman that Jesus will help her. Hope is our great expectancy that we will know Him in all our circumstances, even the seemingly hopeless ones. Hope is this mocked-by-the-world, nonsensical reaching through the crowd just to touch Him. To the cynical, it seems like a waste. *Why reach in such a crowd? Everyone is touching Him. You're wasting your time. What if nothing happens?* We risk great embarrassment to hope in this way, don't we? But the reaching shows something about the woman's heart, something about my heart: a faith undeterred by the world or our circumstances, a faith that believes in what we cannot see. My expectancy grows my heart toward God, grows room in my heart for more of Him, and allows me to see Him here, wherever here is.

Sure, daring to hope feels a little too much like playing with fire, especially when we have been burned before. To hope exposes me, just like the bleeding woman. It lays me bare and vulnerable because I can't fix this and can't control the outcome. My hope puts me right up next to Jesus, torn open and defenseless, completely at His mercy, completely surrendered.

Jesus turns toward the woman. "Your faith has healed you," He says. Her faith that defied the crowd, her faith that ignored the potential humiliation of being caught touching the Son of God as an unclean woman, ignored the fact that Jesus was busy, actually on His way to heal someone of a much higher status, ignored the reports of the doctors who said healing was impossible for her. Jesus saw her faith and it stopped Him.

Toward this woman, *Jesus turns*. And the crowd is big and the cynics are many, but through it all, He knows and He sees her. He knows and He sees me. He doesn't just notice her; He *names* her. "Daughter," He says. He takes my face in His hands, and it is this same word that He speaks over me. "Daughter," He calls me as His own. His gentle voice dispels my fear and assures me that my reaching for Him is not in vain.

Your reaching for Him is not in vain.

I stretch out my arms to Him and realize that He is right here, just two steps in front of me, clearing the way. I push aside the "what if" that would tempt me not to reach for Him. I know who I am and I know who He is, so I must touch Him. The sweet phrases from Isaiah flood my mind: "The train of his robe filled the temple. . . . The whole earth is full of his glory."[2] I reach and I feel that His hem is plenty wide for me to grasp, enough for me and for you and today and tomorrow. Enough to fill and enough to spill over. Jesus turns. He looks into my eyes and sees me and my fear and my hesitation and my sin. "Daughter," He calls me, "faith has healed you. Faith will heal you." He speaks life over all my brokenness, and over all of Betty's, and over all of yours.

His message to us on the cross is the same as His message to the woman with the issue of blood as He stoops down to look into her eyes, to speak to her, to meet her need: "You are worth it." And I want it to be my message to these hurting ones He brings into our lives: You, you are worth it. We are for you. He is for you.

I want my life to be spent chasing after Him, and I want my arms to be filled—not just reaching for but gathering in the hem of Jesus. I want my arms to be filled with gathering His grace, His love, His goodness, His glory. I want to follow Him wherever He is going and be so full of Him that He overflows out of my arms, out of my very life.

Even when it means reaching out my hand with a smile to a situation that might hurt, will hurt.

He gave me the grace to hope before, so I am asking that He would give more grace, again, even if it is harder to grasp this time. Grace to feel joy and grace to hope for life and grace to fight hard, because people are worth the fight. Grace to have arms so filled with Him that they have to remain open and that He spills out. Again I name this place The Lord Will Provide.

In very poor and vulnerable communities, it is common for the suffering, disabled, and sick to be cast out and forgotten. In places where survival is day to day and people are struggling to muster up enough resources to feed themselves and their children, it is unusual to "waste" such precious resources on someone who seemingly will die soon anyway. This is how we found Betty, left alone in her home and essentially wasting away, no longer able to gather enough strength to walk out the door of her one-room house. Her sister from northern Uganda had said goodbye and taken Betty's son to live with their extended family, expecting that she would not live much longer. A concerned neighbor led me to her home, wanting to help but finding herself unable to do much with her own limited income.

Every week a group of women I love gather together in Masese to study the Bible, pray, share stories, and sell their handmade jewelry.

Jjaja Apio and Mary sharing a laugh at our Bible study

Jjaja Nasita selling her necklaces

My girls!

Time for a cooking lesson

Lining up in the kitchen for dinner

Our family table

Our kids acting out a scene from the Nativity
for the children at Amazima

Patricia and me enjoying
the sunflower harvest

Beautiful Katherine

Our sweet Betty

Ice cream in the backyard

Anna, Simon, and me

These two are sisters and best friends.

Our women's Bible study
group in Masese

My friends Lucy, Esther, and Katie

Lillian's love for Jesus
is contagious.

Grace and Patricia with our dear
friend Miss Angelina, who
always makes us feel welcome!

Patricia and me with some of our
guesthouse residents

We had such a celebration for Simon's birthday!

All dressed up for a day in the city!

Children lining up to wash their hands before lunch
at our Amazima Saturday program

Our first students gathered at the Amazima school

Children waiting for
lunch at an Amazima
program in Masese

Chapel service
at Amazima

Seventeen graduates
from our Amazima
sponsorship program
looking toward the
future God has
prepared for them

Benji, the girls, and me taking
communion at our wedding

Our wedding day

I can't believe how quickly these girls are growing up.

Benji and the girls showing off their latest catch

Noah loves his sisters.

Sixteen pairs of feet, plus guests',
means a lot of shoes.

Fun with friends!

Noah brings us all so much joy.

Several hospital visits revealed that Betty might, in fact, recover, if provided with the proper care and a nurturing environment. Truth be told, my heart was certainly not ready for another person of such great need to enter our lives, but I knew that the alternatives were few at best. Though it was not probable that God would heal her, it certainly wasn't impossible. And something had shifted inside me as I processed my grief over Katherine. It wasn't a onetime lesson, and I would need constant reminding of it in the coming months, but God had been so near to us, even though He did not choose to heal her. This time, though I hoped for healing just as much and certainly prayed for it, I also felt certain that God would bring about something beautiful even if Betty died.

Not only had I experienced a new intimacy with God while Katherine lived—and died—with us, I had watched my children blossom as we shared life with this hurting family. They were much less hesitant than I in welcoming Betty. They simply saw her, they saw her need, and they loved her. She never lived in the guesthouse out back but simply moved into our home because she needed help walking more than a few yards. So many times I found a few of the girls curled up with her on the couch reading, singing, or painting her fingernails as if she were a dear friend, which she soon became. Her personality was sweet and gentle, and she fit easily into our household, quietly observing as our noisy and sometimes-chaotic life swirled around her.

I chopped pounds of carrots for stew and taught my children how to read. My little ones lost teeth and library books and shoes. We made cupcakes and played hopscotch and studied world geography. And at night I tucked them all into bed, said good night to Betty, who slept on our couch, hid myself away in the bathroom, and let my weariness crash over me.

As much as I believed we were called to this life of open hospitality, deep in my spirit I was tired.

A few months after Betty moved in, Simon and his grandmother came to live with us as well. They needed a place to stay where they would have reliable access to medical care.

Ten-year-old Simon was a child sponsored by Amazima, and my staff and I had noticed that Simon didn't seem to grow or gain any weight. After Simon endured many different scans and hospital visits, a doctor was able to show us why. We gasped as we realized we were looking at a real, true miracle. A scan of his esophagus showed us that it was almost completely closed, allowing little to no food to pass. In other words, he had lived with a nearly closed esophagus for his entire life. How does a child live for ten years with minimal ability to swallow any nutrients? So Simon began a series of surgeries that would restore his esophagus and trachea back to normal working order.

They arrived in the middle of the night, Simon working hard to breathe through his new tracheostomy tube and weak from the anesthesia of his first surgery. His mother's eyes were fearful, and his grandmother looked downright bewildered. They needed a place with working electricity so they could use a blender to puree his food, a place with quick access to the hospital in case anything might block the trachea tube that was allowing him to breathe. Simon needed daily tracheotomy changes and had to be fed every three hours through his new feeding tube.

Simon's mom decided to leave his grandmother here as his caregiver while she went back to work. They stayed in our guest room instead of the guesthouse out back so that I could help with Simon's rigorous feeding schedule. His grandmother, who we would all call Jjaja, the traditional Luganda name for Grandmother, already seemed tired, and I wondered if she was up for the long road to Simon's recovery that we had ahead of us. It quickly became apparent that she needed massive amounts of encouragement and reassurance that God was indeed in this with her and with Simon and would not leave. I told her that certainly God wouldn't have brought him this far unless He had an unbelievable plan for this little life.

This was the one thing I wasn't sure I could muster, to be the advocate of God's goodness to this woman three times my age, while I fought in my heart for my own hope and also fought physically for the life of the woman now living in our family room. I remembered how much God had used my answers to Mack's questions to strengthen my own faith and prayed that again this would be true.

Just as He had so often provided what I needed without my really knowing or asking for it, God brought two excellent grief counselors into my life at this time. Ironically, I initially befriended this couple in hopes that they could help a few of my girls, but they ended up being tremendous assets to me too, as I had lots more to process than I was initially ready to admit. One day I cried as I closed my eyes and told them of Katherine's death. I told them how I didn't know if Betty and Simon would live and how it was all just too much.

"Tell God how you feel," one whispered. "You can tell Him that you are scared."

I opened my mouth to say the words "I'm scared, God," but they didn't come out. I thought to myself, *No, that's not right. I am not scared. I do not feel alone, and I do not feel frightened.* I searched my mind and heart to identify what I really was feeling. The words came out quietly: "I am tired." And then louder and louder until I was sobbing repeatedly, "I am tired. I am tired. I am tired!"

I stilled myself and waited for His answer. It came quickly, clearly. *I am not,* He answered. *I know you are tired, child, but I am not. I do not grow tired. I will never become weary. Lean on Me, for in your weakness, I am strong.*

I clung to these words as I cared for them: Simon, Jjaja, Betty, my own children. These words were my very breath of life. In the middle of the night feedings and in the countless changes and in all the parenting in between, I spoke these words to Him: *I am tired, God, but You are not. You do not grow weary.* It became my lifeline, this knowledge that He did not feel the exhaustion I did and that I could fall on Him and trust Him to carry me.

Our house was full and our lives were full and I fought weariness, but at the same time I felt energized with great purpose to serve the people under my roof. Even in my weariness, Jesus felt nearer than He ever had before, and He confirmed to me that living and walking in hospitality, even when it was difficult, was His very best for me and for our family. Although I do not long for suffering or trial, I do long for the intimacy with Jesus that comes in difficult times. It is a strange paradox, but there is great purpose in our struggle and pain.

The woman with the issue of blood never would have reached for Jesus so desperately had she not been bleeding. Certainly, twelve years of sickness and being completely ostracized is not desirable, but to have Jesus Himself look into her eyes—was it worth it? Though we would rather be delivered from our suffering and our trials, or never encounter them at all, I have come to long for the tender care of Jesus that feels most tangible in places of pain and desperation.

Really, we are all the woman with the issue of blood; we just have different issues. We grow weary, but He does not. He is the Lord who will still provide even when we are at the end of ourselves. When our energy is spent and our hope is on empty, when our children disobey or our families need more than we have to offer, or we feel like a terrible friend because we just cannot muster the encouragement that is needed,

Jesus sees us and He is not tired. When we are jostled by the crowd of doubts and fears, we reach out for His hem and He turns.

He always turns, dear one. He looks into our eyes and says, "Take heart, I am with you. *I am for you.*"

His hem is wide. And whatever we are facing, He is enough. All we have to do is reach for Him.

12

A FLICKERING FLAME

I SIT AND I WATCH her live. Day after day, Betty's tiny frame lies in one of our guest beds. Her breathing is strained and her heart rate is too slow and still she lives. Her doctors assure us that there is little more we can do. I look into her tired eyes and drop syringes full of juice between her parched lips.

I have been here before. I know how this ends. Wouldn't hope just be foolish at this point?

Yet she lives on.

Four months later, I change her and bathe her frail body, ever decreasing in size. I hold her fragile hand and hope she knows that she is loved. I wrestle. How do I keep asking Him to say yes when I really expect Him to say no? Why would He ask this of me?

I lay my head, heavy, against my strong Father's chest. "I believe in You," I whisper.

It's enough, child, He answers.

I am torn because I so desperately want Betty to be free from suffering. And I am weary from caring for her, physically and emotionally, when it is unlikely that there will be a positive outcome. I'm exhausted from watching her fade. None of it feels fair. None of it makes sense. But I want to be a person who dares to believe big things of our holy God. Faith is believing when we cannot see. And I've been around the block enough to know that miracles *can* happen. I know there is nothing He cannot do, so I pray to that end, even though it is not rational, even though it is not reasonable.

My hope is a flickering flame that has weathered wind and storm. Somehow, God will not allow it to be completely blown out. He sustains me. No matter how desperate things become, somewhere deep inside me He has placed the audacity to hope, the daring to believe that this time, things could be different. It *is* foolishness to hope in a world of death. And God says He has chosen the things that appear foolish in the eyes of the world to bring about His purpose.

This hoping is the exercising of faith.

And she lives.

It is an awkward dance, knowing that He might say no and that I could still trust in the mystery of His plan, yet still expectantly asking that He might say yes. It is blind and it is trusting and it is intimate. Although everything tells me to guard my heart from being disappointed because she is surely leaving this life for the next, I won't give way to resignation, not while she still breathes before me. In this way, hope is my great offering to Him. It is a meager offering, but it is all I have.

All this hope that doesn't make sense? It had become my holy hiding place. On days when I woke up without it, I fell to my knees and asked God to provide it. When I thought I could not bear another minute of watching her suffer, I would curl up in my bed and beg Him for more faith to believe in what I could not see. When I felt the weight of it all swallowing me, I would ask Him to show me where He was and what He was up to, and I would vacillate between full confidence in His perfect plan and fear that I would bury another friend, that another child would be left motherless.

I needed Him desperately, and my need drew me to Him more and more.

In a place where no one could really understand my life or my circumstances, God had allowed a holy loneliness that compelled me to run to Him and confide in Him more than ever before. Surrounded by people who loved me—intentional, thoughtful friends and community members—I often felt completely alone. Because who else can truly and fully understand having so many children with hearts that need mending and tending and growing and healing? Who else can truly understand moving strangers into your home to love them, only to lose them? Certainly, God places each of us in situations that, despite looking on with support and love, others cannot fully understand. In the past year, loss and life had left a big void that only He could fill, and He did. In His presence, I didn't have to explain myself or recount the ordeals of the day; I didn't have to try to describe my feelings in all their complexity. He knew. I didn't have to summon up trite answers or insincere piety. He knew me and He loved me, and I could rest in Him even when my mind raced. He was The Lord Who Provides all over again, giving me a true companionship that no human ever could.

In the darkest night, I was having a love affair with Jesus.

The God of light met me on the hard tile floor of my bathroom, long after the sun had set and the kids had gone to bed, in the place where my story was not what I had expected. God showed me that relationship with Him is so much sweeter than ease and so much better than the plans and dreams I had initially brought to Uganda, to parenting, to my faith.

He was growing in me a fervent, all-surpassing desire for quiet, secret places with Him. He met me in my mess and even in my doubt and assured me that He still desired my obedience and a relationship with me. I learned anew that He loved me truly not because of who I was or what I did but because of Christ and who He was.

"I will give you the treasures of darkness," He whispered, "riches stored in secret places, so that you may know that I am the Lord, the God of Israel, who summons you by name."[1] He summoned me. He called me to come and find rest in Him alone.

Why had I believed my whole life that ease and success, gifts and miracles, smiling faces and my plans fulfilled, meant the Lord's blessing and favor? The blessings also abound in the darkest night and the deepest valley, if we have eyes to see them.

The invitation to experience sorrow and doubt and all those long nights with Him—that *is* favor.

Consider Jesus in the tomb, those three long days in the dark. Of course, the glory of the Resurrection on the third day would overshadow the sorrow of those three days, but God sent His angel to strengthen Jesus at the pinnacle of His anguish in Gethsemane.[2] His heart and His tenderness toward His Son was real that night, long before the sun broke gloriously on the third day.

This was true for me too. He wasn't asking me to hold out for the glory on the other side; He was with me, strengthening me, even now.

The seventeen of us could barely fit around our dinner table, but we squeezed anyway. Family dinner has always been an important daily event in our home, no matter how many are staying with us. I served spaghetti, which usually makes for a humorous and messy meal with all the slurping of pasta.

Simon and Jjaja made most of our dinners humorous anyway. She told stories in her loud and enthusiastic way, and the girls listened graciously even when they were clearly exasperated, wondering when they would ever get a chance to speak. Simon could not swallow yet, being still in the middle of his surgeries, but he always wanted to eat with us. His doctor encouraged him to let us feed him through his tube first and then "eat" his food by chewing it and then spitting it into a bucket without swallowing. I can't imagine what someone else might have thought had they looked in on this crazy scene, and I giggle to remember it, but it felt so normal to us at the time.

After dinner we pushed aside plates and passed out Bibles. Our nightly reading picked up in John chapter 2 with Mary, Jesus's mother, asking Him to save the wedding of friends. "They have no more wine," she states. She knows what He is capable of and comes to Him with confidence. After Jesus responds that it is not His time yet, possibly trying to deter Mary from hoping for a miracle, she looks at the servants in full faith and says, "Do whatever he tells you." Even though His response is not exactly what she wants to hear, she is still confident of what He can do, still certain that He will, in fact, do something.

As we read the story, I heard echoes of my own hopes. I come to Jesus and know what He is capable of. I know that He *can* heal, so I ask for it. And I keep asking. Maybe He will respond that now is not the time for that. Will I believe in His perfect timing? Will I ask for a yes but trust Him and believe that He is working all things for our good and His glory if this time He says no? Do I trust in the mystery of His perfect timing? I desire the confidence of Mary to still say to those around me, "Watch Him. Eyes on Him. Do whatever He tells you," confident of what He can do, expectant and certain that He is still doing something.

Jesus turned the water into wine that night, but not in a grand show of His miraculous power. He did it quietly and only a few saw. "The master of the banquet tasted the water that had been turned into wine. He did not realize where it had come from, though *the servants who had drawn the water knew.*"

Only His disciples and the servants—those who stuck close to Him, who kept their eyes on Him, who did whatever He told them—saw what He was doing. Our God is faithful to reveal Himself to His servants. As we hope in Him, He invites us to see. When we hope and then do not get what we wholeheartedly believed Jesus would give us, an outsider could look and say that we have somehow failed, maybe even that God has failed us. Certainly, the Enemy wants us to feel that way; he tried to tell me daily that if Betty lost her life, death would be the same thing as failure.

But for the servant who is watching, there are always miracles.

This was true for us. Our life was full and our home was full. Yes, there were trials, yet the joy we knew was nearly unspeakable, surpassing what I had thought possible. For me, that was our miracle. He was giving me eyes to see it.

Days consisted of previously unimaginable scenarios: blending a portion of our dinner to push through Simon's feeding tube while he sat with us at our dining room table, happily chewing but not eating; teaching my fourteen-year-olds how to make Betty's porridge and then later how to change her diaper so that I had an entourage of helpers with all hands on deck; bumping into Jjaja as I got up to feed Betty and she got up to feed Simon in the middle of the night and accidentally terrifying each other in our half-asleep state, then bursting into laughter at the sound of our startled screams in the silent house. We nursed our patients and swore when the power went out and we couldn't use the blender to puree Simon's food. Sometimes we just stared at each other through too-sleepy eyes. I laugh now to remember it all and the grace that God lavished on us during an impossible season.

These days and these scenes were so far from what I would have imagined or dreamed for my life, this lifestyle such a far cry from how my younger self would have chosen to raise children and a family, yet somehow, it all felt so right. We learned to revel in the gifts God continued to give as we traveled this rough and winding road together. There was certainly great risk involved, as there always is when we love another, but the joy of life and the sense of His pleasure surpassed the risk immeasurably.

As we opened our lives and our home more and more to the people God brought to us, He made our home a sacred place, filled with His presence and His joy, even in the strain and the hard. I knew that no matter the cost, this lifestyle of love is what I wanted for my family. Even so, I had moments of second-guessing myself, especially as Betty's health continued to spiral downward and it began to look as though we might lose her. Was it right to expose my children to pain in this way? As they continued to pray for her health, I ached to know that I couldn't give them what they were asking for.

But they continued to amaze me with their faith. The girls were not nearly as calculated and cautious as I was; in fact, they seemed oblivious to the idea that some people might weigh the joy of loving someone against the pain of potential loss. They were simply compassionate. They knew how to love and knew that love was right. So they sat on Betty's bed and read her stories, they played (and argued) with Simon as if he were their very own little brother, and they did not turn their faces away when either of our newfound friends vomited, which was a very common occurrence each day.

I wagered that learning to see God in the pain at a young age like this would benefit them. Maybe, Lord willing, they would learn to cling to Him in the inevitable disappointment they would face when they grew up and moved out and experienced for themselves that things don't always go the way we plan or the way we ask of God. I desperately wanted them to know that God was here with us in the sacred dance of joy and pain. I wanted them to have a safe place to grieve and ask all the hard questions and thrash against me and God and, hopefully, by His grace, find Him to be true and faithful, just as I had.

Simon's health improved after a few surgeries. His grandmother was encouraged when he started putting on weight, so they moved out of our guest room and back into their little home a few miles and a phone call away. Betty, too, started to get better. But then she weakened, and that cycle repeated over and over again. Her doctor determined that even the strongest medicines were just not enough this late in her illness. Too much damage had occurred before her treatment began. We began palliative care that would keep her free from pain but not prolong her life.

I read Psalm 63 over and over, the one I had read aloud so many times before Katherine died: "O God, you are my God, earnestly I seek you; my soul thirsts for you, my body longs for you, in a dry and weary land where there is no water."[3] Those words had both pierced me and resonated with me as I held Katherine in her death; I felt parched, desperate, and defeated. But now, different words from the same psalm caught my eye and stuck in my heart.

"I have seen you in the sanctuary," the psalmist continues, "and beheld your power and your glory. Because your love is better than life, my lips will glorify you. I will praise you as long as I live, and in your name I will lift up my hands."[4]

Because Your love is better than life. Yes! Was that it? Was that why He brought us here, again and again? Not because the outcome would be physical, tangible life but so His love would surround us, would engulf us, and we would know that this love is better than life both here and in eternity? We had seen Him time and time again. We had beheld His power and His glory. Our lips could whisper of His glory even here, in certain death, because we had known it to be true, that His love is better than anything we could ever pray for or ask for, life included.

Would we live as though we believed this? Even as we looked at Betty, who might die anytime, would we lift our hands in praise and glorify the Father because of His love, which never leaves or forsakes us?

"My soul will be satisfied as with the richest of foods," the psalm maintains. "With singing lips, my mouth will praise you." Yes, we had known full satisfaction in Him. We would know it again and again. "On my bed I remember you; I think of you through the watches of the night. Because you are my help, I sing in the shadow of your wings. My soul clings to you; your right hand upholds me."[5]

Where are you and I today as we bring our requests to Jesus? Do we hold out our flame of hope no matter how small? We know what He is capable of, and we believe that His love is better than life. Do we ask as though we know? And if we end up asking for something He is not giving, and maybe will not give, do we trust Him enough to wholeheartedly believe He will do what is best for His glory? Will we watch expectantly like the servants and Mary at the wedding, like the psalmist throughout the watches of the night? Will we do whatever He tells us and believe that He loves us and has our good in mind and that we can sing in the shadow of His wings? If so, then we will see the greatest of all miracles: His love for us!

I want to sit near Jesus as I watch. I want to request boldly and then trust intentionally that He will give what is very best for our good and His glory.

~

There is something deeply sacred about knowing and accepting that someone you dearly love is about to die. For a little while, time stands still. You cannot really leave or do or even think about anything else, and so you wait. In those hours, nothing matters except the breath in your lungs, and in hers. All the things we so desperately need to get done are forgotten. All that matters is just *being*, inhabiting the moment fully.

The veil between this life and the next feels thin. Jesus is so close that maybe if we just reach out, we could touch Him, trace the lines on His face with our fingertips. I have never experienced His presence quite as powerfully as I have in the calm and quiet just before He calls someone home.

Betty had been living, and dying, in our home for months. She was on hospice care now and being kept comfortable after multiple rounds of treatments had failed. I would tiptoe into her room and drop water into her mouth with a syringe or change her diaper or just sit in the quiet and stroke her hair. I hummed quietly the words to the song "Healer,"[6] and somewhere in the back of my mind, I did acknowledge that God could heal her, but my wounds were still too raw from Katherine to put much of a voice to those claims. Mostly I just realized that we had done all we could and yet Betty was dying, and I relished the immense responsibility of loving someone well as they prepared to meet Jesus.

Again, we waited. And again, we were expectant. Mine was a different kind of expectancy than I'd had with Katherine: softer, less about me and the plans I had and more about the knowledge that God would meet me without fail. Instead of demanding the thing that I wanted and labeling it belief, I simply expected God to show up, whether through Betty's healing or through her death and passage into new life. I knew now that real hope was my leaning into the arms of God, who would hold me regardless of my circumstance.

The waiting for Him to come and take her dragged on for months longer than any of us expected. Although I longed for Betty to be free of pain and suffering, caring for her was our joy. Life slowed to a crawl and I began to learn again the pleasure and satisfaction of being an ordinary person caring for specific people in a specific place at a God-appointed time. It took hours to spoon just half a cup of milk into her mouth. As the big girls and I took turns feeding her, little sisters wandered in and out of the room or crawled up and down on her bed, curious and unafraid, filled with love that did not know limits. This place was sacred. Jesus continued to affirm that for me daily as I stirred a pot, and checked on Betty, helped with homework, and checked on Betty, folded laundry, and checked on Betty. Sometimes she was semiconscious and I doubt all my checking was warranted, but I was drawn to Jesus in our bubblegum-pink guest room where everything faded away except His face in hers.

Instead of sleepless nights and long days filled with frustration at the waiting, there were hours of peace in the knowledge of His presence here with us. He met me in the stillness. There was something completely beyond my understanding in that time with her, in that room. It was Jesus. He was near.

Children and visitors wrote scriptures on Post-its and covered the wall behind her bed. In the after-bedtime quiet, I would read them to her as if she understood. Actually, I was reading them to myself. I needed the reminder of who God was just as much as she did, and He taught me as I read His Word aloud over my friend.

I don't remember many details of those weeks, just that the presence of Jesus was strong in our home as the days ran into each other in a kind of blur. In the days shortly before her death, He allowed me to witness beautifully miraculous events through new eyes, even though Betty was not physically healed.

I had searched long and hard for Betty's son, who was now living with her aunt. Betty so desired to see him once more before she died. One morning a woman and a small boy walked into our yard. I knew right away as I looked at his face that he was the little boy we had been searching for, and when Betty saw him, she smiled for the first time in several days. They shared sweet moments together before he left again with his great-aunt, who promised Betty she would look after him and love him well.

Another morning my friend Lillian arrived with a large group of men and women from Masese. They had walked nearly six miles to pray over Betty, a rare display of immense love and sacrifice. They had left children at home, missed a day of working or picking on the streets (which was their livelihood), skipped the opportunity to prepare food for the day, just to come show their love and support for this sister and for me. I was humbled and overcome with gratitude for their sacrificial love. Seeing them band together that way lifted my spirits more than anything else could have.

I remember every detail of the night Betty died. I am not sure what had me so certain she was going soon, but I could feel it in the air, and her slowing breath confirmed it. "Be merciful, Lord," was the prayer on my lips, and I knew that He would be, whether that meant life or death. I put the little girls to bed and gathered Margaret and Agnes, two of my oldest, into the pink bedroom with me. I told them that I felt we had a great privilege in being able to sit here with Betty as she was about to meet Jesus face to face. I shared with them my great desire to love her well to the end of her life here on earth and asked Agnes to translate as I read Scripture. I wanted Betty to know that she was not dying alone and that she had nothing to fear.

Slowly, deliberately, I began to read, "Then I saw a new heaven and a new earth, for the first heaven and the first earth had passed away, and there was no longer any sea." I could see it in my mind, this scene described in John's Revelation. "I saw the Holy City, the new Jerusalem, coming down out of heaven from God, prepared as a bride beautifully dressed for her husband."[7] Even with the slowing of her breath and heart rate, Betty glowed, as if she were the beautifully prepared bride.

And I heard a loud voice from the throne saying, "Look! God's dwelling place is now among the people, and he will dwell with them. They will be his people, and God himself will be with them and be their God. 'He will wipe away every tear from their eyes. There will be no more death' or mourning or crying or pain, for the old order of things has passed away."

He who was seated on the throne said, "I am making everything new!" Then he said, "Write this down, for these words are trustworthy and true."

He said to me: "It is done. I am the Alpha and the Omega, the Beginning and the End. To the thirsty I will give water without cost from the spring of the water of life. Those who are victorious will inherit all this, and I will be their God and they will be my children."[8]

Betty breathed softly, peacefully as we read. Agnes repeated after me in the local language, and we all paused to soak in the words and believe they were true. To sit with someone so close to looking upon God's face just might be the holiest of holy ground. To know that we were holding her mere moments before she met the Savior, we felt closer to heaven ourselves. I held her hand, her chipped pink fingernail polish a symbol of how well she had been loved by my children during her time in my home, her fragile fingernails reminders that she would be better off where she was going.

We read, "I did not see a temple in the city, because the Lord God Almighty and the Lamb are its temple. The city does not need the sun or the moon to shine on it, for the glory of God gives it light, and the Lamb is its lamp."[9] I looked around the room at our Scripture-covered sticky notes and at my daughters, the light of Christ radiant in them. Betty's eyes opened briefly and locked on mine, and I rejoiced that soon she would know no more pain or darkness.

> Then the angel showed me the river of the water of life, as clear
> as crystal, flowing from the throne of God and of the Lamb
> down the middle of the great street of the city. On each side of
> the river stood the tree of life, bearing twelve crops of fruit,
> yielding its fruit every month. And the leaves of the tree are for
> the healing of the nations. No longer will there be any curse.
> The throne of God and of the Lamb will be in the city, and his
> servants will serve him. They will see his face, and his name will
> be on their foreheads. There will be no more night. They will
> not need the light of a lamp or the light of the sun, for the Lord
> God will give them light. And they will reign for ever and ever.[10]

And then I read these words, the words of Jesus Himself: "Yes, I am coming soon." And then, "Amen. Come, Lord Jesus."[11]

As the last words of Revelation left my lips, I breathed "Amen," and Betty breathed her last. I held her hand as she beheld the face of Jesus for the first time, and I felt as if I'd had the privilege of handing her straight into His loving arms.

13

FAITHFUL

JUST ONE LITTLE BIRD. She's up when the stillness of five thirty nudges me awake and I struggle to peel back heavy eyelids. She's up and she sings. I wonder how she can even tell that it's almost morning. I wonder why she sings. I walk quietly to the coffeepot and flick on just enough lights to read by so as to not wake my children. Her song is shrill and bold. This is my *quiet* time, and I briefly just wish that one little bird would be quiet.

"It's not light yet. Shhh. *It's not light yet.*"

I lift my eyes from the worn pages of Isaiah, and my gaze falls on Sarah's notebook, left haphazardly on the table after yesterday's writing assignment. She had written about our time with Betty and said that I had courage. I had cried when I first read it, her words about me too gracious, and I'd wondered what courage really is. She wrote that I was brave, but as I sit there in the dark, I think that I am not.

I miss my friends who have gone home to be with Jesus. I know where they are and that it is better, by far, than suffering and sickness. But still, I miss Betty's smile as I wiped her forehead and the way her weak hand felt in mine, her fingernails hot pink from Margaret's tender care. I miss the still, quiet hours by her bedside and the way her eyes understood even if her ears did not. I miss Katherine's laugh, loud and infectious. When I see her children smile, I see her, and I still wish the ending had been different.

Then I see Sarah's words on the paper again: "Our sick friend lived with us for a long time and my mom was brave and took care of her. I saw her praying for her and I know that she was loved and cared for. My mom kept her, and she had courage."

I do not feel courageous. Sometimes I feel downright defeated.

Though we had peacefully said goodbye to Betty and felt certain relief about where she was now, I still had moments when grief blindsided me and threatened to take my breath away.

During the last months of Betty's life, my daughter Sumini had made me a construction-paper flag that read, "You can do it." Her thoughtfulness and simple words made me smile. I hung it above the counter where I kept track of Betty's food and drink intake each day. Now as I passed it, I blinked back tears. The temptation was ever present to think that we didn't do it, that death meant we had failed. But my loving Father whispered a different story. "We did it," He said in that soft Father way, as if it was our secret, as if He could see all the parts of my heart that the world couldn't—all the questions, all the reservations. He heard all my unspoken questions about how things might have unfolded if we had done something different, met her sooner, seen a different doctor, anything. And He assured me that things were always as He intended. "We did it." She is home. She is whole. And we had walked her there, straight into His arms. We had not let go of her hand, and He had not let go of ours.

I asked Him *Why?* again and again. What could all this suffering possibly accomplish? Why would He allow our family to walk through death like this repeatedly? Why would He allow us to love people so deeply?

A dear friend suggested, "Maybe because He knew you would."

Could that be God's answer to us as we walk the hard road? "I knew you would do it. I knew you would love them."

And suddenly the hard road becomes not a burden but a place of great honor, a place of partnership and intimacy with Him. We didn't have to love Betty; we *got* to love Betty. We were allowed by our gracious and merciful Father to love these people, to give ourselves to something so grand as ushering His beautiful children back into His arms at heaven's gate.

Then I think that maybe courage is not at all about the absence of fear but about obedience even when we are afraid. Maybe courage is trusting when we don't know what is next, leaning into the hard and knowing that it *will* be hard, but more, *God will be near.* He is the God Who Will Provide. He will provide His presence, His strength, or whatever He decides we most need. Maybe bravery is just looking fear in the face and telling it that it does not win because *we have known the Lord here.* We have known the Lord in the long dark night.

The little bird sings loud in the early morning dark. And slowly, the sun peeks over the horizon.

While homeschooling later that day, I ask my daughter Joyce for her definition of courage, and she says, "To have faith." Maybe that is just it. Though we tremble and feel uncertain, courage means we press into a God who is certain, sure, steady. He carries us; He lifts our heads. And His unfailing love and comfort become our courage and our hope.

Days later it is raining. The huge drops pelt our tin roof so hard that we can hardly hear ourselves talk, but as the rain slows, I make out a familiar noise and I laugh. The same little bird that cannot contain her song too early in the morning is now singing through the rain. I wonder where she's hiding and how she can keep singing in this storm. I wonder why she sings. The rain slows to a trickle and the sun peeks from behind the clouds, and suddenly all I can hear is her glorious song.

To have faith, I think. And I wonder, *Does she sing because she knows the sun is coming?*

And I want to be just like that little bird.

Hope is a crazy thing, a courageous thing. Faith is a bold, irrational choice. But that little bird—she feels the sun coming, knows with certainty that it will come, even when she can't yet see it.

We live in a world where innocent people suffer and good friends die and stories don't have the endings we pray for. The pain and hurt are everywhere. But the joy and hope that we find in our Savior? They are everywhere too. I do not have all the answers; actually, I don't have many at all. But this is what I know: God is who He says He is. And in the hurt and the pain and the suffering, God is near, and He is good, even when the ending isn't. Our pain does not minimize His goodness to us but, in fact, allows us to experience it in a whole new way.

God brings to mind Mary of Bethany, who chose the greater thing by putting aside her tasks to sit at His feet. A natural doer of tasks, I always resisted putting aside the daily rhythm and necessities of life to sit in His presence, until He made my life such that it demanded this. I could provide my friends and family with food and shelter and medicine and love, but I could not give life. And a longing for the lives of Betty and Katherine had forced me into desperate time at His feet that I had come not only to cherish but also to long for desperately. I craved that middle-of-the-night time when I would sit on the floor of my bathroom, just me and Him. Night after night I would sit and imagine myself, like Mary, washing His dusty feet with my tears. Even a month after Betty's death, our guest room and our couch were without occupants, but I often chose quiet time on the bathroom floor because I had felt His presence so strongly there in my struggle. It was there I had first heard Him whisper in the nights after Katherine's death, "Come." And so I kept coming.

I think more about Mary of Bethany—her ability to know what was good in the eyes of Jesus and her ability to question Him at the same time. I think of a different conversation between her and Jesus, four days after her brother, Lazarus, died. She had called for Jesus days earlier, when her brother fell sick, and only now was He entering their town. "Lord," she said, weeping, "if you had been here, my brother would not have died."[1] She blatantly voices her disappointment. *Where were You, Lord? Didn't You hear that we had called for You? Why didn't You come?* I remember hours spent in my tiny bathroom, pressing my knees into the floor and choking on my tears. "Where are You?" was my heart's cry. "It's not fair. I called on You. Why didn't You come through?"

I imagine Jesus, who wept with Mary. I imagine the tenderness in His eyes as He looks into hers, knowing fully His great love for her and knowing fully the outcome she does not expect. I imagine that same tenderness in His eyes toward me and those long nights and the way I could feel Him holding me, strong in my flailing. I remember how I never felt that He was condemning me for my anger, disappointment, confusion, or tears but rather that He was weeping with me, whispering, *I know, I know, this is not My design. This is not the way I intended it.*

Jesus is faithful to Mary. "I am the resurrection and the life," He tells her sister, Martha. "Do you believe this?"[2] And there in her mess of emotions, she knows Him. So have I. I have known deep in my spirit that He is who He says He is, seen the tenderness in His eyes toward me, felt His strong arms carrying me when I could barely go on.

John says, "Jesus loved Martha and her sister and Lazarus. So when he heard that Lazarus was sick, he stayed where he was two more days."[3] *So.* He loved them and *so* He didn't move immediately. He loved them and *so* He allowed Lazarus to die. He tells His disciples that He is glad He was not there so that they, too, may believe. He did this for me too. He showed Himself to be a God who uses delay to grow my belief and strengthen my relationship with Him. He loves me and *so* He allows me to feel pain that draws me to Him.

Yet in the very same breath that I say that I trust Him to purpose all things for my good and my growth and His glory, I can attest that He weeps with me. It's a bit strange, if you think about it, that Jesus weeps with Mary. Surely, He isn't crying because Lazarus is dead. *He knows what He is about to do.* He knows that Lazarus will be dead for only a few more minutes. He weeps for His friend. He weeps with His friend. He sees and knows the outcome of my situation. He knows what He is doing, even in the endings I don't expect, and still, in all His compassion, He weeps with me for a world that is not as He intended, for sorrow that He did not design. Jesus wept, and the crowd said, "See how he loved him!"[4] Oh, how He loves us!

I can sing because I know what is coming. I can hope because I know *who* is coming. In the dark of the night, I have seen His face, and I have known His promises to be true, and I know the Light is coming.

I want to be brave enough to hold out the hope of the Gospel to a world that is hurting and alone and afraid. Not a hope rooted in the absence of pain or heartache or suffering. Not optimism that looks for the best-case scenario or happy ending. A true hope that rises from the full assurance that our Savior is on His way.

It's not light yet, but I know Him, the One who is the Light.

And so in the dark, I will sing.

After months of putting life on hold to care for Betty, I suddenly found myself feeling a bit empty, purposeless.

I would tiptoe into that pink room again and again. I knew she wasn't in there. No one was in there. But her presence lingered, and my hands longed to serve her, to change her, to wash her. My eyes longed to look into hers again, and my heart longed to see her shy smile. My longing for His presence surpassed all these things and He met me there. The more I sought Him, the more and more I found Him. As I knew Him increasingly, I loved Him more and more. Isn't this always the way?

In the days before Betty died, I felt that the Lord spoke the same word over and over as I sat by her side: *faithfulness.* This, a fruit of the Spirit for all who believe in Him. This, something He has promised me. And so I asked Him to show me what it was. *What does it mean, Lord, to be faithful?*

In the days after she died, I walked into her room a thousand times out of sheer habit and remembered words often attributed to Aristotle: "We are what we repeatedly do. Excellence, therefore, is not an act but a habit." It struck me. Surely, faithfulness is not a onetime act, not a decision or a destination, not something to eventually be attained. Faithfulness is what we repeatedly do. It is a habit formed of long, hard obedience in the quiet. Faithfulness is dropping milk through a syringe for hours into a mouth that could barely swallow in the middle of the night. Faithfulness is pursuing that resistant teenager again (and again and again) even though she yells and hurls ugly words. Faithfulness is in chopping carrots and folding laundry and all the things that go unseen and unnoticed. Faithfulness is in a million tiny decisions and a million small surrenderings—submitting with a simple *Yes, Lord*—that create a lifetime of obedience in the extraordinary and in the mundane.

In walking through the everyday routine with my girls and the few extras God placed in our home, He had taught me what faithfulness really meant: that it was in the long nights of staying awake just so Betty wouldn't be alone. That it was in the repeated prayers for her health and her peace and her comfort, even when no one was looking, even when no answers were coming. That it was in every dropper full of milk, every scripture that was read, every hymn that was hummed over her sleeping head. As it turns out, faithfulness was in the ordinary, in the everyday things that do not feel glorious but, in fact, lead us to His feet.

Friend, faithfulness is what we repeatedly do, whether or not we see the results. Faithfulness is when we pour into hard people over and over, when we continue to serve in difficult situations, when we intentionally choose to lean into Him in our troubles as well as our joys. Faithfulness is a habit formed in our hearts when no one is looking, when the day is done and the stars creep out and our call isn't easy but we don't turn away.

And ultimately, faithfulness is truly and fully found in the One who pursues us though we thrash against Him, who sits with us as we wait in the silence, who fulfills all His promises with a yes and amen in life everlasting.

God's faithfulness to me in this season went above and beyond comforting me and helping me find a new song of hope, though that would have been more than enough. Quietly, He was fulfilling another part of His perfect plan for me and my family. In a season of my asking the Lord to open my eyes to His miracles and His goodness, He had opened my heart as well.

Benji was a young man who like me had originally come to Uganda on a short-term volunteer trip but felt God tugging his heart to stay, specifically in long-term men's ministry. Now living full time in the town of Jinja, he faithfully led Bible studies with small groups of men throughout the week in the hopes of discipling them toward Jesus and pouring Christ's love into their lives and families. In his free time, he lent himself as a jack-of-all-trades to the many missionary families and young singles in the area, willing to help in any way needed, fixing plumbing and troubleshooting the Internet and anything in between. He had been a friend to our family ever since he arrived in the area, but during the past several months, I had wondered if maybe he could be more. I had been observing him quietly for quite some time as he led a Wednesday night Bible study for young adults that I participated in, fixed my children's bicycles in the backyard, and discipled men like Mack, whom I cared deeply for but whom I knew would benefit more from a male teacher who could help him dig into the Word. I admired Benji's willingness to do seemingly anything to help anyone, and I greatly respected his faithfulness to continue pursuing difficult men in ministry. Benji lived what he said he believed. I couldn't think of much that would make a man more attractive.

Benji had asked me out twice, early in our friendship, but I had made it clear I wasn't interested in dating. I had long ago made peace with the fact that an intimate relationship with anyone other than Jesus was probably not in the cards for me. My lifestyle was unconventional, my children were many, and I'd found a rhythm that worked, at least most of the time, for running my household on my own. Plus, now? Life was so full and sometimes fairly chaotic. I didn't have the capacity to devote time to another person, and with all the emotional energy I was investing in my girls and in other people God brought our way, I couldn't imagine having enough left to pour into a romantic relationship.

But Benji had been a comforting presence throughout the past few years, checking on the girls and me often, helping in any way he could. He loved people well and deeply, without seeking any credit or recognition. Occasionally, I could see a tenderness in his gaze toward me or one of the girls that somehow reminded me of the gentleness of Jesus. As I continued to see Benji's heart for the Lord quietly on display, God seemed to be prompting me to consider him in a new light. The problem was, I had so adamantly declined his previous invitations that I knew he wasn't ever going to ask again. I valued that he respected me enough not to push the issue, but as my feelings about him changed, I wasn't sure how to reopen the conversation.

I prayed for months, waffling between hope that there really could be something between us and incredulity at the thought of anyone truly being interested in a serious relationship with someone so committed to so many other things. Still the thought persisted and I felt the Lord's gentle nudge forward. I second-guessed myself. Was this really the Lord or just some crazy whim? Could something more than friendship really develop between us? Finally, after listening to me go on and on about it for months on end, a trusted friend said, "Well, either it will work or it won't, but at least you will know. If you are still thinking about it, it is probably worth the risk." What she said wasn't some profound biblical truth or even the audible voice of God I had been secretly hoping for, but it was right. So I asked Benji to come over for coffee early one morning, and after hours of small talk in the still-dark quiet before the girls awoke, I nervously shared my heart: that I'd been wondering if we could get to know each other more intentionally. The words came out so jumbled that I wasn't even sure they were comprehensible, but he said he would think about it.

After much prayer, we both made the decision to start seeing more of each other, intentionally. My life didn't really lend itself much to dating, so we each learned the other's heart and history during breaks from homeschool and during late-night trips to the hospital to check on friends and hours of dinner preparation for a tribe of growing, hungry children. We found other ways to eke out a bit of time together. I broke things intentionally so that I would have to ask him to come fix them, and he suddenly needed to use our washer much more than usual. In all of our interactions, no matter how small, I saw faithfulness in him—a faithfulness God had been teaching me about in this season, a faithfulness I wanted more of in my own walk with Him. Slowly, God began doing something so foreign in my heart. Where I had always been a leader, I desired to look to Benji for leadership. Where I had always wanted to make decisions my own way, God started carving in me a desire to seek out Benji's opinion before making key decisions, because his wisdom was apparent. I wanted to follow this man as he followed Jesus. I wanted it more than I had wanted anything in a very long time.

After months of seeing each other quietly in this way, we sat under the October stars, and the wind rustled leaves on the trees and I felt deep peace.

"I'm going to ask you to marry me one day," he said, looking straight into my eyes, as if he could see through them and into my heart.

"I think I might say yes," I whispered.

14

Time to Sing

My feet pound loud against hard pavement, and sweat drips
from my brow. This rhythmic pounding soothes my heart, helps me to
daily process all that God is doing in and around me. Sometimes as I
run, I listen to worship music and forget that I am running and lift up
my hands and attract all the stares. Today I just listen as the pounding of
my feet breaks the still silence of the sweltering afternoon. It has been a
longer than usual dry season in Uganda, and I feel that it has been a
longer than usual dry season in my life and ministry, with all the sickness
and loss and sorrow for those I love.

Simon has moved back in, this time with his mother, Anna, who has
put her life and career on hold to care for him. His medical care has become increasingly more complicated after many failed surgeries, and
Anna and I have bonded over faulty tracheostomy and feeding tubes,
long hospital waits, and our shared desire to pour ourselves out for our
children and love them well, although their current needs are vastly different from each other.

They've lived with us again for many months, and now, after what sometimes feels like an endless season of hospital visits, an endless season of pleading for Simon's young, fragile life, he is facing his eleventh surgery. Anna, who has become my beloved friend and confidante as together we laugh and cry over this beautiful and hard journey of motherhood, is understandably weary. I am too. We have watched and prayed through ten failed surgeries already. *Ten.* A real weight of exhaustion has settled over both my heart and hers. Will he *ever* get better?

The air feels hot and dry, and so does my spirit.

But I feel God's love so strongly for me here, and I know with all certainty that the long dry season has drawn me to Him in a way that I never could have known apart from it. In the stillness and the quiet, in the suffering, I had fallen in love with Jesus all over again.

And only then, only after I had felt His piercing gaze of love for me, had He brought a man whom I was indeed falling in love with as well. A change was happening: this thing that I thought might never happen, a man beginning to feel more like part of our family, more like someone I couldn't ever imagine life without. Slowly and certainly, God was weaving our hearts together, and I was both thrilled and terrified.

The Lord was using Benji to unlock a place of deep, unbridled joy within me, one that I had not allowed myself to experience in quite a while. Interspersed between long nights of helping Anna with Simon and grieving over the loss of others we had served were moments of uninhibited laughter and closeness with this man whom I was ever so slowly falling in love with. Benji would sit and laugh with Grace and Patricia as we all snapped green beans for dinner, or joke with Margaret as he taught her to ride her bike. One time I had been rolling out pizza dough as Scovia walked through the kitchen, and in a moment of silliness I reached out and left a flour handprint on her cheek. This prompted her to put flour on my nose right as Benji walked into the kitchen, who, in my defense sprinkled flour on her head. Mere minutes later, I stood doubled over with laughter in the kitchen, without any more flour to finish our pizza dough, as Benji and the girls were now throwing it all over each other out in the yard. I was in awe of the joy the Lord was providing for us, even in the midst of such a difficult year.

I felt hesitant, even scared, to fully pursue this relationship, though it had brought so much delight to both me and my family. I had become accustomed to having Jesus as my only sufficiency, my only confidant, the only person from whom I sought any affirmation. It had been a sweet season—just me and Him, in it together. I think I was afraid that I might lose that closeness with the only One who had ever really known my heart.

I had prayed Isaiah 61 over my children since they came home, "to bestow on them a crown of beauty instead of ashes, the oil of gladness instead of mourning, and a garment of praise instead of a spirit of despair."[1] Now, after the girls were tucked snugly in bed, Benji and I would sit on the couch and he would sing these words over me: "Beauty for ashes, can you believe it? Beauty for ashes, can you receive it?" I knew deep in my spirit that this was my loving Father's song over me too. Beauty for ashes, can we believe it? Beauty for ashes, can we *receive* it? *Receive,* He said. Could I?

I slow my run to a walk. I remember a verse from Song of Songs that God has recently been speaking to my heart. I feel as if it is His promise to me now.

My beloved spoke and said to me,
    "Arise my darling,
    my beautiful one, come with me.
See! The winter is past;
    the rains are over and gone.

Flowers appear on the earth;

    the season of singing has come,

the cooing of doves

    is heard in our land.

The fig tree forms its early fruit,

    the blossoming vines spread their fragrance.

Arise, come, my darling;

    my beautiful one, come with me."[2]

Maybe He is calling out to me, inviting me into a new, different season. And though I step with trepidation, it is safe to go with Him. It is safe to run to His arms, regardless of where that might lead me or what I might encounter.

I turn to run home. The horizon begins to change with evening coming. There is dinner to be made and homework to be done and baths and bedtime and all of it to do over again tomorrow. Suddenly, the sky darkens. As I run, I feel a drop of water hit my forehead. One, then two, then a slow trickle. I stop. It begins to pour, and I stand and catch the rain in my hands.

Just like that, Uganda's long dry season is over, and I hear His voice steady and clear, *Behold. I am doing a new thing.* As sudden as the rain, I know His promise over us this season: that the winter is past and the dry season is over and He will again make all things new. Flowers will appear on the earth; the season of singing has come. I tip my face up and rain washes over me. His mercies, new. His peace, constant.

I weep as the rain soaks me on this stifling day. I know the water is the Lord's clear message to my heart, *Refreshment is here.* Rain. A season of joy. I know this deep in my heart, yet I am hesitant. His voice speaks to me, clear in a way that it seldom is, and I know He is asking me to step into a season of great joy with Him. *I am bringing blessing and refresh-*

ment on your life, He says. *It has been a long, hot, dry season. I know, child. But that season is over; refreshment is coming. Step into it. You can enjoy the rain. You can receive what I am giving with open hands and rejoice.*

After a seemingly endless season of hard, I need permission to rejoice. If I am honest, maybe somewhere along the way I have forgotten how to truly rejoice in Him. Here again, He is calling me to hope, this hope that appeared impossible when the world was hard and dark, this hope that has taught me so much of His heart for me.

I feel a nervousness, maybe even a fear, in stepping into a season like the one I sense He is promising me. I have grown used to the dry season. I have known Jesus here in this long, hard place, and rainy season now seems foreign. But I can feel Him assuring me that He will be known here too. *Receive,* He says again and again. *Receive My blessings; receive My provision; receive My love for you.*

Song of Songs continues,

My dove in the clefts of the rock,
in the hiding places on the mountainside,
show me your face,
let me hear your voice;
for your voice is sweet,
and your face is lovely.[3]

Again and again in the days to come, the Lord would confirm that He was calling me out of the cleft of the rock—that He was giving me a new song to sing, a beautiful song arising from the places of dust and ashes around me. It was a song of praise. He was calling me to step into all He had for me here. It was time to come out of the hidden place and sing and embrace all that He was giving, the blessing He was pouring out. And He knew that my voice might come out crackly and tired at first, out of practice. But He would hear beauty in my song of praise in this new and glorious season.

I hold my hands open to the rain and promise that with open hands, I will believe in new life and I will receive joy.

I finish my run and return home to find Benji and Hellen sitting on the roof of his car playing Scrabble, undeterred by the rain. My heart smiles.

Months passed, months full of the same, even in this season that I felt God had declared "new." I taught homeschool lessons and put away laundry and reminded children to wash their hands. Benji fixed the girls' bicycles and sneaked them candy and left love notes in the coffee maker for me to find in the morning. I was still involved with some ministry outside our home, mostly in Masese, as well as caring for various people living with us in need of help and restoration. Simon continued to require constant assistance, and he and his mom had settled comfortably into the guesthouse out back while they waited for next steps from Simon's surgeon. Anna and I became fast friends as we shared chores and stories and our trials and joys.

On a warm May evening after dinner, Benji took the girls out for ice cream so that I could have some time to just be quiet before the Lord. Unbeknownst to me, they were making some pretty big plans.

A week later, our best friends offered to keep the kids so that we could go on a date, something we had been making time for more often as things between us grew more serious. We sat on a picnic blanket overlooking Lake Victoria and the Nile River, the water aglow with lanterns from local fishing boats. We talked and laughed about everyday life in ministry, and my heart welled with thankfulness.

Benji poured a basin of warm water and washed my feet, a kindness he had made something of a tradition early in our relationship but that still left me speechless each time. I marveled at this man, an extension of God's tenderness toward me.

He began to read from Song of Songs chapter 2, "Arise, my darling, my beautiful one, and come with me." I choked up as he began to speak over me the very words that God had been speaking to my heart. "Show me your face, let me hear your voice; for your voice is sweet, and your face is lovely." He assured me of his love for me. He prayed that God would always protect our relationship from the "foxes that ruin the vineyards" that might steal our joy.[4] We each were the other's beloved. And with tears in my eyes, I nodded my head before he had even finished asking it, asking if I would be his wife.

Wild shrieks of glee streamed from the nearby cluster of trees, and soon we were ambushed by shouts and hugs and kisses from our sweet girls, who had been hiding in the bushes all along. Many of them began speaking all at once, rehashing the plan that they had made over ice cream earlier in the week, all of us astonished that little Grace and Patricia had both kept the secret. Tim and Shana, faithful friends who had been our biggest support throughout all our relationship, smiled as they looked on.

After the commotion from the girls died down a bit, Tim and Shana took them home to prepare a dessert celebration, and Benji and I stayed behind for a few minutes to pray. We prayed again the words from Song of Songs, asking God to protect our union and strengthen us as we grew together. We prayed over each one of our daughters. We gave thanks.

And as we headed home to enjoy ice cream with those we love most, a gentle rain began to fall.

15

HE WHO PROMISED

EVEN THROUGH THE CHANGES of this season, some things remain unaltered. Out in the backyard, past the garden where the sunflowers grow tall, past the mango tree where the kids climb wild, our small white guesthouse is full again: three bedrooms that the kids and I painted, a small toilet and a sink, and the closet where we keep the girls' bikes.

I often find myself drawn out here. In my very own yard, I get to bear witness to people from all kinds of places recovering from all kinds of setbacks and moving toward what God has for them next. Someone to bear witness to our stories is what we all long for: sick people who have been discharged from the nearby hospital but still have no place to rest, homeless families looking for jobs or some means of support, people waiting for surgery or recovering from addiction or just waiting and hoping that someone will see them and lock arms with them and say, "You aren't alone here in this big, scary world. We see you. We will be your people." Here in our yard, we bear witness to the stories of people. And here, we bear witness to God. People have been loved to new life here, and some have been loved straight into the arms of Jesus.

Again, in a season of new, God has invited our family to wide-open hearts and deep compassion, to participate in healing and hope. In the quiet of the evening, after I kiss cheeks and tuck bodies warm into beds and pray over sleepy little heads, I sneak out to the backyard and watch new life.

Simon and Anna are still here, waiting on the eleventh surgical attempt to repair his esophagus. In the room next door, Yusufu, a man who recently found himself homeless after an illness caused him to lose his job, is staying with his two young children, Mariam and Shafik. On the other side, two single moms, Alice and Maggie, along with their two small children, share a room. Alice had been partially paralyzed by a stroke and left to die by family members who were afraid and did not understand her condition. Maggie, her tiny twenty-year-old body ravaged by AIDS, had nearly died alone in her home when she miscarried and could not stop bleeding. For her first weeks with us, I hadn't let her stay in the guesthouse because I was too afraid to lose her. Instead, after blood transfusions from the local hospital, she would sleep in my room on a mattress on the floor.

This evening I sit on a small stool, watching these people we have come to love dearly, and read the words of Hebrews 10, those I'd painted on the wall of the guesthouse a few weeks earlier, a reminder to our guests but really a reminder to me: "He who promised is faithful."[1] Yes, He had been. And He would continue to be.

Anna graciously cooks beans over a small charcoal stove on the cement porch outside her room, as our backyard residents usually prefer to eat much later than our family does. As the only one of our guests who is truly "well," Anna has taken it upon herself to cook not just for herself and her son but for everyone staying out here. She knows the ropes at our house after having lived here for several months, and she is a great help to me as we serve our many new visitors together. Yusufu helps his children wash their hands in preparation for supper, and they jump around in happy anticipation of their meal. Alice sleeps on a small couch curled up next to her three-year-old daughter, Lotuke, and I realize how tired she must be from a full day of physical therapy to help her relearn to walk. Maggie smiles brightly at her son, Sam, sitting in her lap as they wait on food. And I marvel. Beauty from ashes. I don't just know it to be true; I get to live it. We get to watch redemption take place; we get to reach out and touch it; we get to be a part of it.

And then Maggie groans that her stomach hurts. In a moment, my mind takes me back to a different place at a different time with Katherine, whose stomach had hurt. I remember us at the hospital and they are telling us that there is nothing they can do. I slowly watch her get worse and worse. I hold Katherine's hand and read from the book of Psalms, and she breathes her last. I feel fear creep into my heart as I return to the present and look at Maggie. She could die. So could Simon. We could find ourselves there again, waiting expectantly but still uncertain of the outcome. I reach out to hold Maggie's hand, and it looks so similar to Betty's, a hand I held not too long ago—a hand I held for hours that turned into days and days that turned into weeks until finally I got to place her hand in the hands of Jesus as He took her from this earth. I remember the way Simon hugged me when he and Anna first moved back in and he learned that Betty had died; he had watched me care for her and had seen my hurt and discouragement. I blink back the fear. It is just a stomachache. I glance again at the words on the wall, bringing to mind the rest of the verse I have memorized: "Let us hold unswervingly to the hope we profess, for he who promised is faithful."[2]

I can trust Him. I can hold on to hope because I can hold on to Him.

I feel it stirring in my heart, the strange mix of pain and excitement, a combination I will experience again and again as each of our friends here transitions into the new life, outside of our home, that God has planned for him or her. I think of the privilege it is to be able to speak life over these hurting people and believe in new life for them as we strive to love them the way we've been loved by Christ—the privilege it is to watch His faithfulness unfold in their stories.

I sit there in the candlelight, thirteen growing young women sleeping soundly in our home a few yards away and all kinds of lives being transformed before my eyes. I sit, and I remember the Lord's faithfulness. I remember His resurrection. Life from death. Beauty from ashes. Beauty from the torture and the nail scars and the blood-red life spilling out everywhere. Beauty from the black of the tomb.

Our hope is in Him, and this hope is never in vain.

Weeks after that evening, after Simon's eleventh surgery failed too, his surgeon, one of the best in the country, explained to us that he just didn't think Simon would get better in Uganda. Though this hospital had the most experienced surgeons and highest-quality equipment Uganda had to offer, the doctors couldn't always get their hands on the specific things they needed for a successful outcome. The surgeon suggested that if Simon's life was indeed to be saved, we would need to seek other options.

So we pursued visas and medical appointments in the United States and watched in awe as God flung doors open wide and orchestrated everything perfectly to get him there. Blessing poured out as Amazima quickly raised the money for Anna and Simon to get to the States, and very generous surgeons offered to operate on Simon free of cost. Friends and family members willingly opened their homes to them. I would be able to fly with them to the States, but with my girls at home in the care of friends, I could not stay for the full duration of Simon's recovery. None of us could believe the speed and ease with which we got Simon and Anna all set for the long journey to the United States , usually a daunting undertaking.

That very month, Simon squealed with delight as he, Anna, and I took off on his first airplane ride, and more than thirty hours later, I laughed at his mother's wide eyes as we entered the Atlanta airport. Their friendship had blessed me deeply, and to travel this journey with them was my great honor. It was a strange and great joy to watch my biological family welcome members of our Ugandan family into their home and to witness the love that Simon and Anna received everywhere we went.

I sat in the Vanderbilt Children's Hospital waiting room just a few days after our arrival on US soil and let my tears of gratitude fall while I waited for Simon to come out of surgery. I could hardly answer when a nurse approached to ask if I was okay. I was so much more than okay, so in awe of God's provision. In the wilderness of our fear that we might lose yet another friend, He saw us. He saw Simon and every small detail of his esophagus and his journey and his little heart.

Later, Anna and I quietly entered the recovery room, where we found Simon sleeping peacefully. The doctors felt nearly certain that the surgery had been successful and that this time Simon's esophagus would remain open, though it would take a few months to know for sure. The compassion of the nurses was astonishing to both Anna and me, as we had grown so accustomed to the overworked nurses in Uganda, who were usually exhausted and having difficulty keeping up with all their patients. Here we had a nurse all to ourselves—it was almost unbelievable!

I spent a few days at my parents' house with Anna and Simon as Simon rapidly recovered. Within a week, he was scarfing macaroni and cheese and hot dogs as if there had never been anything wrong with his ability to swallow. Anna and I laughed at all the stark contrasts between American life and our lives in Uganda: the absence of dust on paved roads, the oddity of huge houses with very few people inside, and way too many choices at the grocery store.

Simon needed to stay in the States for several months to ensure the success of his surgery through follow-up appointments and possibly a few additional minor surgeries, so I left Simon and Anna in the care of my parents and close friends while I headed home. It was surreal to Skype my parents from Uganda upon my return and see Anna and Simon jump on camera to tell me that they were making a birthday cake for my grandmother. Our worlds had been bridged in such a sweet and intimate way.

Then months later, in the quiet of the evening, I opened my computer and found an e-mail that announced that Simon's surgeries were finished and had been fully successful. I stared at the screen while it sank in. Attached were confirmation numbers of his plane ticket home to Uganda. He was coming home, finally healed. Amazima's dedicated staff members looked at me incredulously when I shared the news the next day. None of us could quite believe that this years-long journey was coming to a close. We had been fighting for this both physically and in prayer for so long, and it seemed almost too good to be true. My girls and I started to count down the days until Anna and Simon returned. It felt as though our family members were coming home.

I saw their car pulling up before it got to the gate and I tried to contain my excitement as they dragged themselves out after the long journey. But in seconds we were a ball of arms and legs as we embraced each other, giddy. The girls were screaming and Simon was laughing and Anna and I both were crying into each other's shoulder. I could just barely hear her whisper, and it gave me goose bumps in the blazing African sun. "He did it," she said quietly. "God saved my son's life." And she sobbed.

Yes, He did.

They stayed for a few weeks while they got readjusted, Anna jumping right back in where she'd left off, helping me love and serve the many who were still calling the guesthouse home. And then nearly a year and a half after that first sleepless night they and Jjaja had spent with us, they drove away from our home smiling and laughing, arms excitedly waving out of van windows as my children chased them down the driveway, waving just as hard. I stood in the driveway and let the tears of joy well up in my eyes. They were well. *They were well.* God had made Simon well. And it had been a very long time since I had been a witness to a story with *this* kind of ending.

I stood in their room long after they left and ran my fingers over the words of Hebrews painted on the wall: "He who promised is faithful." I felt that Simon's life had been a promise to me: that God was still good, that He was still working, that He still saw our family stopping and loving the ones He put in front of us and trusting Him with the endings and believing Him for good.

So many others had lived here too: Katherine and her children; Betty; Nalongo and her twins, Babirye and Nakato; Isaac and Teokol and their little Lodengo; Jjaja Gwanoni; Zulaika and her family; Maria and baby Agnes; and so many more. The list rolled through my head and went on and on. I saw all their faces and I laughed and I cried. I sat down on the floor of the tiny bedroom that had held so many lives; I sat and I remembered. I know the truth of these words now in a way that I didn't when I first wrote them on that wall. I didn't know what it would cost me to hold unswervingly to my hope or just how difficult that would prove to be. But it was true then and it is true now, and it will continue to reverberate throughout all eternity: He is faithful to us.

I thought of the sad stories and the happy stories and all the stories in between that had flooded this place. We'd experienced both successes and failures, though I was learning that even what I called failures were full of God's purpose. We'd witnessed endings I would have classified as good and others I would have called terrible, and everything in between. But through it all, the one constant was this: He is faithful.

It is twenty months after Simon first came to live with us, after the first of his esophageal surgeries. We are celebrating his twelfth birthday in my backyard with more than fifty staff members and friends, but my heart is celebrating a victory so much bigger. His little life, faithfully restored, feels very personal, a gift from Jesus, an earthly testimony to the eternal hope He has been teaching me.

I think back over the past year and a half and remember all the times Simon's grandmother and I ran into each other in the middle of the night, clinging to only Jesus as we tried to nurse our loved ones back to health. At times, we both thought we might die of sheer exhaustion, and I lost count of the times things went wrong—the moments of sheer panic over his young life.

Yet here we are on his twelfth birthday. We've packed our home full and I've made spaghetti with a million meatballs, and all the staff members and friends and family who have been on this intense journey gather around to celebrate Simon and Jesus and life. Simon happily blows out the candles on his chocolate birthday cake. His mother's words echo in my mind: "God saved my son's life." He did. And I look around at all these faces, all these people we love coming together to celebrate, and I know that *He saved mine too.* He has given me treasures in the darkness, indeed; He has brought beauty from ashes, time and again.

Today, Simon can swallow food just as well as any other twelve-year-old and play soccer with the best of them. He's gone back to school and Anna's gone back to work, now a social worker on staff with Amazima. They wash dishes and do homework and laugh and sing and pray in their own little home, just as we do here in ours. I give thanks. I allow myself to remember just how crazy *hard* it all was, just how *long* it has been, just how *tired* I have felt, and just how *faithful* God has been to each of us through all of it.

The others have left or are on their way out now too. Yusufu recovered from tuberculosis and got a job on a farm nearby to support his family. Before we knew it, they had moved into a little house, and the children began attending school again while their father went to work each day. Slowly but surely, Alice relearned to walk and regained almost all function on both sides of her body. She and Lotuke moved back to Masese, where they had lived before, and astounded friends and family with their health. Maggie and Sam would eventually move out as well, Maggie's strength and health now such a stark contrast to the frail, desperate woman who moved in so many months ago, the woman I had feared we might lose.

People ask me how we do it—all these people living, and sometimes dying, in our home. Most days I have no idea. Lots of days it's just downright hard. Some days it is more than exhausting. But I look at Simon, at his mother, at my children. My eyes meet Benji's over the long picnic table, and we smile. I look at all these people here gathered under the stars to celebrate life, and I am reminded of why we keep opening our doors and our hearts. God is who He says He is. He is here with us in the hard places and the happy ones, when things go as planned and also when they don't. Our hope in Him is not determined by our circumstance but by His character, always faithful to us.

We name all our places, the good and the hard, The Lord Will Provide, and we hope and believe that He will. Our hope is never in vain.

16

A Deep and Quiet Love

I WATCH MY DAUGHTERS walk ahead of me down the hardwood aisle, pink dresses swishing on the floor. *When did they get so grown up?* I hear His words, "They will be called oaks of righteousness, a planting of the LORD for the display of his splendor,"[1] the scripture that I read over them last night, the scripture I have prayed over them for years, and I think of all the ways He has made His promises true for us.

And today all the more. I hold my daddy's arm tightly and lock eyes with the man at the end of the aisle, the man who will become my husband just minutes from now. I am not nervous. I am ready.

This man, so much like Jesus, has quietly pursued my unruly heart. He found me in the mundane moments of snapping green beans and stirring soup and coloring on the floor with my five-year-old, and he began to learn my heart on purpose. And just as I fell wildly in love with

God in quiet minutes of ordinary life that He made holy, my falling in love with this man had happened in the still of the morning over coffee before the kids awoke and in the quick glances across a rowdy dinner table.

I stand at the end of the aisle and I can feel it, this ushering into the holy grace of God, again. A new calling even beyond that which He has already given: to join my life fully with another, fully believing His promise that this would make me more like Him. "Lord, You are good, faithful, and true," sings the guitarist as I put one foot in front of the other. And He is.

Love took me by surprise when I had all but given up on any notion of romantic love in my life outside of my relationship with Jesus, and marriage was a dream I'd long ago laid aside for the reality I knew He had called me to.

Up until recently, love had been loud in my life: a crying foster baby, a raging alcoholic in need of care, the screeching laughter of children, and the clatter of pots and pans after dinner. I had felt God in the monumental decisions of adoption and foster care and in guiding the launch and running of a ministry. I had seen and known His goodness in the big: a move across the world, and a rapidly growing ministry and family. But lately, God had been teaching me to fall in love with Him all over again in the quiet and the small: the still minutes after bedtime, the monotonous beauty of routine, the endless peeling of vegetables and wiping of noses and folding of laundry. God was teaching my heart to be still before Him, to feel His power in the breath of the wind and the cool of the evening and the everyday duty of shaping hearts (mine too!) to be more like His own. His beauty and His faithfulness were just as real in these moments, His goodness to me just as tangible.

Benji embodied this kind of quiet, faithful love. So when he asked me if I would marry him, there was no doubt in my mind that this was the man God had designed to shape me more and more into His image. This invitation to a lifetime of human companionship was my heavenly Father more beautifully illustrating His love for me than He ever had before, and it was only the beginning.

I walk down the aisle and we make vows to each other, vows we will break, both imperfect sinners found in Christ and desiring to be more like Him. We take communion with our girls as well as our closest family and friends. We break the bread; we take the cup. The Lord Will Provide. The Lord has provided. I marvel that after He gave His own Son He would still give this: the joy of building a family together, the blessings of everyday life. Who is this God who loves us so tenderly? I know in this moment that I have only begun to scratch the surface of understanding His extravagant love for us.

And this love wasn't just for me. The girls and I had woken up early on the morning of the wedding, knowing there was lots of hair to be styled, many pairs of earrings to put in, and more than a dozen bows on dresses to be tied. As I peeled open my eyes that morning, I heard fifteen-year old Ellie shout from the next room, "I'm getting a DAAAAAADDDD!"

And as I watched this new dad dance goofily with our girls at the reception, picking up the littlest and twirling her all around, my heart swelled with joy at all that God would accomplish in my daughters' lives through a tender and Christlike father. He had not only remembered the desire of my heart but had seen their needs as well. This love was for them too.

For years, I have prayed Isaiah 61 over my family, asking the Lord to give beauty from ashes, asking Him to indeed grow these daughters of mine into oaks of righteousness for the display of His splendor as I felt He'd promised to me all those years ago. I have cried tears straight onto the words "freedom for the captives" as I begged this promise for my little ladies. I have rested in the promise of the oil of joy instead of mourning, and I have rejoiced with the prophet Isaiah as each one has come to her own understanding that He has clothed her in garments of salvation and a robe of righteousness. My eyes stuck right there on Isaiah 61, praying those words in verse 11 that the Lord would cause righteousness and hope to spring up before all nations.

Only on Saturday morning, the morning after I married the most Christlike man I have ever met, did my eyes wander past verse 11, down the page to chapter 62, as if now that I was beginning this new chapter of life, maybe God would give me a new chapter to pray over my family. My breath caught in my throat as I saw these words that I had somehow never noticed before.

> The nations will see your vindication,
>> and all kings your glory;
> you will be called by a new name
>> that the mouth of the LORD will bestow.
> You will be a crown of splendor in the LORD's hand,
>> a royal diadem in the hand of your God.
> No longer will they call you Deserted,
>> or name your land Desolate.
> But you will be called Hephzibah ["my delight is in her"],
>> and your land Beulah [meaning "married"];
> for the LORD will take delight in you,
>> and your land will be married.
> As a young man marries a young woman,
>> so will your Builder marry you;
> as a bridegroom rejoices over his bride,
>> so will your God rejoice over you.[2]

Right there on the thin gilded page was His heart for me, for Benji, for each of our daughters, for our family: that we would know His delight in us, the way He rejoices over us. And now He had given us a very real illustration of the joy of a bridegroom over his bride.

The past few years had been a season of quiet, of darkness and sorrows, of joys that felt too personal to share with anyone other than my heavenly Father. I had been learning the beauty of the secret place, just me and Him. The Lord who knows my heart had long been whispering to me of a new season, and my flesh worried that this new season might take me out of my secret hiding place with Him—that somehow a physical, tangible relationship with another might take away from my relationship with my Builder, my Lover, my Life Giver. It felt scary to say goodbye to the season God had used to make me who I am.

But actually, it became just the opposite. Benji, a faithful husband, would be God's tangible and daily reminder of His delight in me. This relationship would only enhance my perspective of God and my communion with Him. I imagined that marriage would be good, but I never could have imagined that it could be this holy. I did not understand that I would melt under this man's gaze, so full of the love of the Father for me, and that all the more each day, his grace and his patience would speak to me of God's unconditional love. I didn't imagine the way his delight in me and our children would so mirror the way the Father delights in us—how Benji's constant pursuit of us, his unrelenting desire to know our daughters, would provide a daily picture of the pursuit of our God. I have watched him faithfully love and care for us in so many ways, from simple things such as preparing breakfast each morning without fail to elaborate dates involving a movie and fancy restaurant in the big city, a few hours away. I have watched him press in when a daughter spoke hurtful words or withdrew from his love, and I've seen him reach out instead of away when I tried to take control into my own hands. My husband's love is another way that God has chosen to pour out His extravagant love on me and on our family, another constant reminder that He rejoices over me and over each one of our children.

I have watched my girls come alive under the loving gaze of their father; I hear the delight in their voices as they call him "Daddy." And without my hardly even asking, God has given me my new prayer over them: that in knowing the delight of their earthly father, they would begin to grasp all the more the delight of their heavenly Father; that they would be a crown of splendor in His hand; that they would grasp this new name He promises, "my delight is in her."

Our God is good, and He gives good and perfect gifts and good and perfect words to us. His delight is in me, in us. May our delight be evermore in Him.

17

HOME

TWO MONTHS LATER, WE took our honeymoon in Israel. We walked the ramparts and sipped coffee and saw Scripture come alive. I spent much time contemplating the land that Jesus once walked and reflecting on all the ways He had been at work so tangibly in our lives through recent years. There had been so much pain and wrestling, yet there had been such unimaginable joy. The first few months of marriage had been a big adjustment for our family, as we had expected. Although it was wonderful, it certainly was not without struggle as we all got used to our new normal. But daily I was reminded that it was worth it. To be in the place we have been given, with the people we have been given to love, it is always God's gift to us, and it is always to His glory, even when it might not be what we once expected for our lives.

In the daily struggle, in the shepherding of our daughters' hearts and the pursuit of them even when they pushed against our love, in my ugly sin that was exposed anew with my beloved now sharing every part of my life, I heard God continue to whisper to me, *I am not done yet.* And I knew that His promise was that He was doing a new thing, in our family and in me.

I considered all this as I sat on a rock with my toes in the Sea of Galilee. I thought of Peter, who was fishing on this water when Jesus called to him for the first time, called him out and away from the mundane and ordinary, away from the life he had known, and asked him instead to be a fisher of men, to follow Him.[1] Did Peter know what he was getting into? Leaving his simple, familiar life to step into something that would lead to this unexpected, radical life with Christ? Did he see it coming?

On this same sea, Peter became so afraid of the storm that he panicked, forgetting all trust and faith, forgetting all the miracles he had seen, all the times the Lord had come through. Then the Lord called him to walk to Him, to trust Him though it did not make sense, to believe in the face of the impossible, to reach for His hand. Peter faltered, but Jesus did not. Peter battled trepidation and began to sink, but he reached for the One who saved him from the waves and who would save him again.

Then I imagined him sitting here where I was, in his little stone house on this vast and beautiful seashore after Jesus's death. Three years of miracles on this water. Three years of meals together and waking and sleeping and life. Did he wonder if it had all been a dream? Surely he longed for his friend, his teacher. Just a stone's throw away was the synagogue. Did he wonder if the Pharisees had been right? Did he wonder if everything the disciples had known and hoped for in Jesus was destroyed, if their hope had been in vain?

I bet his mind raced with the memories the way mine does when we have lost a loved one. I think of all those we have loved and lost, and I remember the most unexpected details: the shape of their hands, the feel of their skin, the sound of their cries. I bet he pictured the dirt under Jesus's fingernails and the gentleness in His eyes and the curve of His sandals and the lilt in His voice, and I bet he just ached with missing Him.

And so Peter went fishing. What else would he do? Back to the ordinary, back to what he knew. Did he think of Jesus out there on the water? All those memories flashing before him as they do when something so all-consuming and urgent is suddenly ripped away and the one you loved is seemingly gone for good? Did he even notice above the chatter of his friends and the torrent of his thoughts that there were no fish in his net? Did it even matter?

But there on the shore stood a man. And he said something vaguely familiar: "The other side!" He called above the waves, "Throw your nets on the other side!" Can you imagine the twinkle in Jesus's eyes before they realized that it was Him? And as the nets filled up, the blinders fell off. "The Lord! It is the Lord!" they rejoiced.[2] I pictured Peter wildly jumping into the water, splashing, swimming, running, sopping wet into the arms of his beloved Savior, his friend.

This is how I have known Jesus. In the normal day, in the ordinary and mundane, He simply and gently calls me to Himself. In the dark night, in the howling wind, when I am alone and afraid and all my trust and faith seem far off and lofty, He is there, offering me His hand, walking me through the impossible. I falter, but Jesus does not. And in those still, quiet moments when I wonder if it was all just a dream, when I wonder if the world was right and my hope was in vain, when I wonder what I was even thinking, there is His voice, warm and familiar, and I know, "It is the Lord!" My Savior, my friend—He is near.

This is how He wants us to know Him: Friend. In the routine of the day and the dark of the valley, in that which is terrifying and that which is familiar, He revels in drawing near to us, in revealing Himself to us. Can you envision how, with that twinkle in His eyes, He said to His disciples, "Come and have breakfast"?[3] As if it was just another ordinary day, as if His desire really was just to be near them, to spend time with them. Even after their wealth of fish caught—153!—He had bread laid out for them to eat, abundance. He broke it into portions, just as days before He had broken His body for the world, and He called them to eat, just to be with Him.

He has broken Himself just for this—that we might partake, that we might be near to Him.

Even after the abundance He has given us in His body broken on the cross for our sins, the only true and acceptable sacrifice, His resurrection saving us for eternity with Him, He calls to us now to join Him. He calls to us here in our ordinary every day, desiring to give us even more, inviting us to taste of His goodness, to reach out for His hand, to walk in His footsteps. Desiring to commune with us and just be with us and us with Him. He wants to be near.

Months after we return home from Israel, we find ourselves bouncing on squeaky taxi seats, the dry Karamoja dust flying up from the dirt road to coat our faces and mat our hair. The noisy and excited chatter that filled the vehicle as we departed at three o'clock this morning under a blanket of stars has died down, as all the other passengers have been lulled into a restless sleep by the heat of the afternoon sun and the jarring of the van on the rutted road.

Benard, our friend and coworker, beams. He is excited to have Benji and me on this trip with him, and we are honored to be making the twelve-hour-long trip up to Karamoja with seven elderly people we intend to return to their homes. Some married couples and some single, each of these jjajas had been sent to Jinja for medical care, or what was perceived by relatives at home to be "a better life." Yet upon arriving, they were confronted by the harsh reality that life in a slum near a town center is *not* the "town life" that they had envisioned, medical care is not free or readily available, and the lifestyle of these shantytown communities is not at all similar to the village way of life they are accustomed to.

Without access to work or money, each of these individuals had been unable to afford their bus ticket back to their homeland and so found themselves stuck, some for a few months and some for many years.

Mabel, an elderly woman from the bunch, had been sent down to Jinja by relatives who believed that someone there would be able to "fix" her blindness. She kept a young woman's baby during the day in exchange for a corner of the woman's twenty-square-foot hut and a pile of rags to sleep on. I remember the first time I visited her, being shocked that she was sitting inside in the pitch dark during the middle of the day, before I realized that she couldn't see. She cut up some leaves she had gathered to boil for her lunch while she told me how she longed to embrace once more the daughters and sons she'd left behind but knew she probably never would.

Juliette lived with her husband just a few yards down the hill. They had come to Jinja to seek out the "better life" they had always heard of, but instead they struggled just to survive. Juliette, who was unable to walk, spent her days sitting on the little dirt step in front of her house, often just staring blankly. When local children ran past and kicked or threw rocks at her, she simply turned her face away and sighed. At the end of the day, her husband would come home with their livelihood: scrap metal he had picked from the trash heap that he would sell for enough shillings to buy just one jerry can of water. On a good day, he would bring home a handful of rotten vegetables from the same trash heap for Juliette to prepare for their one meal.

The others had similar stories, all stuck in a foreign way of life, unable to get home to their places and their people. Benard had befriended these individuals during his daily ministry in the community, and one day he eagerly declared his plan to Benji and me: "I have this idea," he said, "to take them home."

Home. It is such a profound and enormous blessing that I so often take for granted. A place to call our own, a place to be known, a place to belong. I think each of us at our very core longs for a place to call home, perhaps because our hearts were designed for our ultimate home in heaven. I could certainly understand their longing to return to where they felt they belonged, and I loved Benard's heart to want this for them as well.

Benji and I both voiced concern that maybe these people would not be welcomed back into their homes. Day-to-day survival is paramount in the Karamojong culture, and extra mouths to feed and bodies to care for can often be seen as burdensome. These elderly people had ostensibly very little to offer. They would need care and support once they got back to where they had come from. We certainly didn't want to drop them off in places where they would not be accepted, where their lives might be even worse than the squalor and hopelessness of their existence in Masese.

Benard and a skilled team of social workers spent months tracing the families of each individual and making sure they did, in fact, have places to go home to. They asked many questions to ensure that anyone we helped relocate would be welcomed and well cared for. Then they spent weeks more preparing each person for the journey, and now finally the day had arrived. Still, I was skeptical. Would they really be received despite having almost nothing to contribute?

My fears that these people would be rejected quickly slipped away. At each stop, our elderly friends were embraced by family members who had been waiting all day for them to arrive. Sisters, brothers, children, and friends proudly helped us carry our passengers' belongings as they led us to their new homes, places that had been prepared for them in advance.

I watched two sisters who hadn't had contact in years embrace. They became like giddy teenagers as they jumped up and down in each other's arms. With tears in her eyes, the elder sister said to me in the local language, "I did not expect to see my sister again before I died!"

Another young woman raced to our van as we pulled up and nearly dragged her blind mother out of it. Her mother had been gone only a few months, but to the daughter it had seemed a lifetime. There was a large meal prepared and she eagerly showed us the place where her mother would sleep.

The last stop of the day was Juliette's home. The terrain leading up the manyatta, the group of huts surrounded by a protective thorn enclosure, was too uneven to cross in the van, so we parked about a kilometer away, barely able to make out the thorn enclosure in the distance. Because Juliette was unable to walk, we decided that we would carry all her and her husband's belongings to the manyatta first and then come back for the elderly couple.

As we approached, loaded with her few bags and bundles, excited friends and relatives led us to the small, round hut they had prepared for Juliette and her husband, the very same hut in which she had raised her children. We turned back to the van to get Juliette, but we made it only halfway. I could hear them before I could see them, shrieking and singing with excitement and laughter.

As we drew closer, I could see that three other grandmothers had run ahead of us to the van and were excitedly welcoming their friend and sister. As I watched from a distance, they scooped her up and plopped her into a wheelbarrow to carry her back toward their home. As they wheeled her toward us, her eyes shone with an inexplicable joy that comes only when one realizes he or she is deeply loved.

Not only was Juliette received, she was cherished. Her friends and sister were so thrilled to have her home that they couldn't wait a few extra minutes for us to get her out of the van. Her husband walked a few steps behind the wheelbarrow party, beaming with pride at the celebration taking place around his beloved wife.

We watched happily as these women acted like young girls over their reunion with an old friend. Juliette might have had "nothing to offer," but it didn't matter. *They wanted her.*

The sun faded in the evening sky, and I watched Juliette, radiant in her purple dress, being bounced away from me in a wheelbarrow by her dearest friends. Juliette, who had survived by eating other people's trash. Juliette, who had been despised and ridiculed by the children of the village, who turned her face away as they hurled both stones and insults. Here, she was somebody to be honored and celebrated and known. She was someone to be carried, someone to welcome eagerly, someone to celebrate.

She was home.

And I imagined heaven.

I bet it is a lot like this, I thought. All of us, with nothing to offer. Yet we'll be cherished, celebrated, delighted in. As a child, I pictured heaven with golden road and pearly gates, a fairyland filled with flowers. But now I wonder if maybe it will be a lot more like a vast open savanna and a bumpy dirt road and a wheelbarrow.

We have nothing to offer, yet here we are. And there Jesus is, arms open wide, reaching for us as He always does, though we have nothing to offer Him but ourselves.

I look down at my feet, filthy from this day of trekking through dust. I feel the sweat drip down my brow. I will show up to heaven like this too. Worn and dirty from the effort of giving all I have. Scarred from loving deeply, living fully, hoping wildly.

And I see the way Juliette's eyes shine as careful hands lift her out of the wheelbarrow and place her on a woven grass mat, the place they have so tenderly prepared for her. I've known the Lord's care and tenderness toward me and know that one day we will experience it all the more fully.

I see Jesus, beaming at His beloved bride as the angels celebrate.

Can you picture it? You, banged up and bruised, nothing to offer, and Jesus, smiling at the object of His magnificent love—receiving you, welcoming you home.

"No eye has seen, no ear has heard, no mind has conceived what God has prepared for those who love him."⁴ Could we dare even try to imagine?

I think of those who have gone before me: Katherine and Betty, others we have loved. I think of them being welcomed into the gates of heaven by the saints, eager and excited to have more join them in worshipping the Father. I close my eyes and picture the body of believers in heaven, and they are not what one would expect. They are the Mabels and the Juliettes. They are the Peters. They are the homeless man, the drunk, the leper. They are you and me—raggedy and worn, scarred and dirty, not the kind of people one expects to find in the presence of a King.

Yet we are received. More, we are celebrated. And we bow before Him and we worship.

We are home.

18

BREAD OF LIFE

IT IS RAINY SEASON AGAIN. My friend Tamara and I slip and slide down the muddy hill to Masese, where weekly we study the Bible with a group of women who have become so dear to us. These women make jewelry that is sold by Amazima, providing a source of income that has allowed them to put aside other harmful forms of work such as prostitution, alcohol brewing, and picking through trash. Every Tuesday we come, joyful and overflowing, or broken and weary, or anything in between, and we don't have to hide it, because these women have become friends. We wear our babies on our hips, and we wear each other's burdens. We break bread together in each other's homes, and each week we sit in a circle in the dirt space between falling-apart slum buildings and crack open His Word, desperate for His filling, searching for His wisdom, inquiring together, "What do You have for us, God?"

It is beautiful, when I have eyes to see. It is beautiful, but my heart isn't prepared for Masese today.

I scuff the dirt under my sandals and let my mind wander as the women share prayer requests, each more devastating than the last. Last week, just two days after I held her baby in this very circle, our friend had been poisoned and died abruptly. We shake our heads in disbelief and try to remember the good things she brought to this community. But as we continue to share, we learn that someone else's mom is slowly dying of tuberculosis and another's daughter was assaulted. Far too many people have fallen prey to alcoholism and addiction, and we see the way this so quickly destroys the lives around us. *And how do we not lose hope?* I wonder. I let my mind wander because I am weary. I don't want to engage in this kind of suffering again today. I live just a few minutes away from here, but my life is still so different. My hard looks like teenagers with rolling eyes and fragile hearts that are crushed with a few wrong words or glances. The hard things in Masese are rampant disease and rape and murder. I haven't spent enough time with Jesus, and today I just can't seem to open my heart to that kind of hurt without feeling despair.

I force myself to kneel down in the dirt and lay my hands on a sick friend to pray. My hand is wet and I realize that she is letting her tears fall, vulnerable, in front of me, in front of our Father. Her hurt is different from mine, but really we each are just as in need of a Savior as the other—both willing Him, begging Him to come quickly. I ask Him to open my heart to right here and right now. I ask Him to make Himself known.

We sit in the dirt and let the tears fall. And despite my best efforts to harden myself to the suffering today, faithful God breaks me, gives me eyes not just to see the pain but to know it intimately. These aren't just people. These are my friends. These are people I know, people He knows. I know their names, their husbands, their children. He knows each hair on their heads and the deepest cries of their hearts.

I allow myself to imagine us in the palm of His hand. I imagine His tenderness as He numbered those hairs, and I imagine Him looking into these women's eyes and smiling, delighted in His daughters. I close my eyes and in my mind I hear the voice of my husband as he sits on our bed and strums his guitar. "For mercy, for comfort, we wait on the Lord," he sings.[1]

Today I feel as if we are just waiting. Today *hope is something we fight for.*

A woman I don't know very well walks by our circle. I have heard stories of her. She sits on the ground against the wall of the little dirt church we meet behind and stares vacantly. Nobody is really sure if she is disabled or if she has just been abused by so many men that she doesn't talk anymore.

Another woman, who I know well and love dearly, stumbles down the hill and nuzzles her head into my shoulder. She lived with us years ago as she recovered from alcoholism and her child recovered from terrible burns, but today her drunkenness is obvious as she tries to communicate with me through language barriers and slurred speech. My eyes look into hers, bloodshot, and I plead with her. She is such a good mother sober. I ask where her little girl is, trying to remind her that being home alone is how the child got injured last time, but she isn't listening. She kisses my cheeks and stumbles away.

We circle back to the subject of our friend whose body, just days ago, was lowered into the ground after she was heartlessly killed, intentionally poisoned. One week ago she sat in this circle with us, and now her body lies buried while we try to figure out who will care for her babies. The women look defeated. I feel defeated.

How do we find the hope of Jesus here? How do we proclaim that He is at work when we just can't see it?

Let us see You here, Lord, I pray desperately. He answers with Romans 2:7: *"To those who by persistence in doing good seek glory, honor and immortality, he will give eternal life."* These women, they persist.

Against all the odds, when it would be easier to just give up and go ahead and call this place hopeless, they cling to their hope in Jesus and persist in doing good. They persist in seeking His glory.

I trudge back up the hill with my mind full of questions. *God, where are You in this mess?* As I ponder, my foot slips and lands in a mixture that is surely part alcohol and part human waste. I choose to call it mud. As I begin to sigh, *of course,* two strong arms wrap around me from behind and my friend Santina's laughter fills my ears. She is laughing at me because she knows how distracted I was and of course, *of course,* I stepped in the mess. She grabs my arm and drags me to her home, where she pulls off my shoes and scrubs them in a basin of soapy water. Water isn't easy to come by around here, and I can't believe she is using it on my sandals. I beg her to stop; I'll wash at home. She proceeds to wash my feet. She is washing my feet and I want to protest, but I think of Jesus, bent down, towel around His waist, instructing Peter, who just doesn't understand. He whispers to me, *See? Do you see Me? I am at work here.*

My stubborn heart may not always want to believe it, but I know that it is true. He is at work here. I think of the Israelites. God Himself had faithfully protected them as death fell upon the firstborn in all of Egypt. With their very own eyes, they had watched Him part the Red Sea so that they could walk across on dry land. But when they found themselves in the desert, the first thing they did was begin to grumble. "We should have remained slaves in Egypt!" they cried.[2]

Like them, I have personally known His faithfulness time and time again. God has kept His promises, throughout all my life and throughout all of history. I have tasted of His goodness; I have lived in it. Does it take just one hard day to forget?

The Israelites stumbled miserably through the desert. God had such good in store for them, but they just couldn't seem to believe it. And as they voiced their doubt that God would come through, He whispered a new promise to Moses: "I will rain down bread from heaven for you. The people are to go out each day and gather enough for that day."³ I am struck by this. *Just enough for that day.* Isn't that what He gives us? Provision, His sweetness even in the barrenness of the desert.

The Israelites looked, and they saw the glory of the Lord coming like a cloud. Thin flakes of bread, *sustenance,* covered the ground, and they looked to each other and asked, "What is it?" this abundance that they did not even recognize. "It is the bread the LORD has given you to eat," came Moses's answer.⁴ And for forty years the Israelites ate manna. Every morning it appeared. Every evening it melted away. Each day, each person found that he or she had exactly the amount that was needed, no more or less, just *enough.* Enough.

When I once more head toward home, Maggie walks up the hill in front of me. Having witnessed me slip, she is giggling about my feet and my grumpiness. Maggie, who I once thought would die. Maggie, who at twenty years old held her four-year-old and her dead baby and bled all alone in her house with no one to help her. Maggie, who moved in with our family just as frail and sick as Katherine and Betty. Maggie, who slept on an extra mattress in my room for weeks because I was so afraid of death that the couch seemed too far away. Maggie, who *lived.* She walks up the hill, her arms full of necklaces that she now sells through Amazima to provide for her and her little guy, both happy and healthy back at home in this community, and her heart full of God's Word, which she loves to share with others. *I am at work here,* He whispers again and again. *Can you believe Me? Can you believe My promises?*

Of course I can. I later read these words of 1 Peter: "You have tasted that the Lord is good."⁵ I cannot deny that I have tasted of His goodness. I cannot deny that I have seen and known Him working all things for the good of those who love Him, even the ugly, hard, unspeakable things. I have tasted manna, *enough for today.*

For mercy, for comfort, we wait on the Lord. Our certain hope is found in Him.

~

Months later, I sit in the drug-and-alcohol-rehabilitation unit of Uganda's only psychiatric hospital and pretend to be comfortable on the cold, hard metal chair. I can't imagine how people get better here. I hold the trembling hand of a dear friend who has walked this road before, who has been victorious over addiction for years until this recent relapse. I am devastated. *Relapse* is such an ugly word. I know how truly it is our nature. Though addiction is not my challenge, I too relapse to my own dreadful ways. I too know victory only in Jesus and desperately need His grace to pull me out of my patterns of sin. For a moment, I hate this place, our broken humanity. I hate this struggle for my friend.

He sees me start to cry—not the subtle, silent tears I've learned to muster during situations like this, but big, ugly tears with sobbing and snot running down my face. I turn away to compose myself and let my strong husband take the lead in conversation. I know I need to be strong for our friend, but I am too sad. This place is too sad and we are too broken. Our children hold a birthday cake, waiting expectantly for the celebration we came to bring. He is much sicker than we thought we would find him, and I want to shield even them from this hurt and disappointment. We sing "Happy Birthday" anyway.

"Pray for me," he says. "Prayer. Prayer will make me well."

I reel. I don't want to pray. Not to a God who lets this happen to people. *Not this.* I think. *Not this, God. No, God.* All those thoughts that I know I'm not supposed to think, that I know He has proven wrong before, swell in my mind again. *Your plans are not good, God. Look at this! Your plan is a mess. No, thank You. This is not what we signed up for, and this is* not *okay with me.* I am the addict and doubt is my drug, this ugly lack of trust, the place I turn when I am weak. It is my lifelong Jacob wrestle, my unwillingness to lay a dear one on the altar and trust that the Lord will provide. I, who have spent years learning to live the yes, fight back a flesh that screams no to this plan. *Why can't we have the happy ending, God? We've had so few. Please, could it not end up a mess this time? Could we* not *end up in rehab?*

The girls pass out cake.

Though my wrestling is the same as it was years ago, His grace allows me to hear His voice much more quickly now. All those quiet moments alone with Him in the dark have given me an affinity to hear Him still in life's noise. *Listen,* He says. My friend is asking for prayer. A man who ten years ago cursed God and knew nothing of His Son, Jesus, asks us to pray for him to the One he knows can make him well. *He knows Jesus.* We are here again, in rehab, but it is different this time. We are *His.*

I realize I never would have sought God's face and known Him in the way I do today if I hadn't walked my own desert road, starving for more of Him. I see and testify to His grace and goodness in the suffering in my own life. Do I believe He'll offer that same grace and goodness in the stories of those I love? This isn't how I would write it. But I have known and seen again and again that God writes the better story. God sends the manna, all that we need, even when we do not understand it.

We drive the long road home, my questions still swirling and God still answering and my spirit still wrestling and my Father still assuring. How do I live when I don't see the miracle? When I don't see the ending, when I don't know the outcome?

I think of the disciples headed to Emmaus after Jesus's death. I cannot imagine the disappointment they must have felt. They'd left everything they had ever known and spent years of their lives following this man, believing they'd have the happy ending they thought He was promising them. Instead, they watched His gruesome death: betrayed, beaten, and killed. They had seen Him remain silent, seemingly powerless against the authorities, doing nothing to save Himself. This certainly wasn't their idea of a happy ending, wasn't the ending they had been waiting for. I imagine their hopelessness, their disbelief. *We thought we knew who He was,* they must have thought.

"As they talked and discussed these things with each other, Jesus himself came up and walked along with them; but they were kept from recognizing him."[6] It doesn't just say that they didn't recognize Him; they were *kept from* recognizing Him. I wonder, did their hopelessness blind them? Were they blinded by their own despair, as I have been, lacking in trust?

Yet in their hopelessness, *Jesus walks beside them.*

Jesus asks them what they are talking about and they can't believe He doesn't already know the story. They explain their sadness and convey their raw disappointment: "We had hoped that he was the one who was going to redeem Israel."[7]

We had hoped.

Even the testimony of the women, their close friends, isn't enough to convince these disciples in their despair. They walk on. And Jesus, so gracious, doesn't chastise them for their doubt but points them to the Word. "'Did not the Messiah have to suffer these things and then enter his glory?' And beginning with Moses and all the Prophets, he explained to them what was said in all the Scriptures concerning himself."[8] Oh, how I wish Luke had also recorded this part of the conversation—Jesus Himself, illuminating His very own Word and story for them! But the even more miraculous revelation of the story is recorded.

As they approached the village to which they were going, Jesus continued on as if he were going farther. But they urged him strongly, "Stay with us, for it is nearly evening; the day is almost over." So he went in to stay with them.

When he was at the table with them he took bread, gave thanks, broke it and began to give it to them. Then their eyes were opened and *they recognized him,* and he disappeared from their sight. They asked themselves, "Were not our hearts burning within us while he talked with us on the road and opened the Scriptures to us?"

Then they got up and returned at once to Jerusalem. There they found the Eleven and those with them, assembled together and saying, "It is true! The Lord has risen and has appeared to Simon!" Then the two told what had happened on the way, and how Jesus was recognized by them when he broke the bread.[9]

Sometimes, I walk the road that God has assigned me like these two walk that road to Emmaus. If I let it, despair can blind me. In sneaks doubt and disbelief as I explain what I perceive to be broken promises: *I had hoped . . .* I have thought these bitter words, choked on them even. And in the midst of it all, Jesus walks along beside me. My preconceived ideas of what He should be doing and what would be best leave me blind. My hopelessness and my own doubt prevent me from seeing all Jesus is doing and, worse, blind me to Jesus *right next to me* and all around me. But really, does my heart not burn within me? When I really look, really pray, I know that He is here, that He was here all along.

Sometimes I think I know how God *should* act, what He *should* do, but instead He wants to walk the road with me, to point me back to Him, to reveal Himself to me. Even when I do not recognize Him, He illuminates the Scriptures, reminding me of all He has done, all those promises kept, and all He has yet to do. Haven't I known the whispers of His glory in all this suffering? I have.

"He took bread, gave thanks, broke it and began to give it to them. Then their eyes were opened and they recognized him."[10] He was known to them in the breaking of the bread. *Communion.* He gave thanks and He gave them bread, and when He gave it to them, they saw. A few nights before, this same Man had broken bread in the same way, saying "This is my body. Take. Eat."[11] Like the Israelites, that which they did not fully understand, still fully satisfied. Jesus, this fulfillment of that age-old promise that the Lord will provide. In the desert. In the wilderness. In my doubt.

He reached His hand across that table, the hand that had reached out to them in the storm, the hand that had reached to heal the sick and the sin ridden, a hand that had been nailed to the cross. He reached His hand out across that table and they knew Him.

Our van creeps toward home and I close my eyes in the dark and imagine Jesus reaching out to me, to us, to our friend in the rehab unit. In the thanksgiving, in the communion, in the willing receiving of that which may still be mysterious to me, I know Him. Here we are, called to His table. Called to communion with Him, called to fellowship with Him, to receive and to know.

"They got up and returned at once to Jerusalem."[12] At once! I imagine the stark contrast in their seven-mile journey to Emmaus and their journey back to Jerusalem. They walk (or run!) the same road, but this time the hope and excitement is palpable. "We have seen Him!" they announce.[13] "It is true!" All that He has said, all that He has promised, they have known it to be true. *And haven't I?*

I have been to Emmaus. I have walked the road pocked with doubt and despair and the wondering and the *I had hoped* and the lie of Satan that maybe this time He let me down, that maybe this time He would not be enough. But when I push aside those lies, I can say with full con-

fidence to you and to anyone who cares to listen, "I did not walk alone."
We do not walk alone. God, in His unimaginable grace, walks beside us,
whether or not we choose to recognize Him, reaching for us, offering us
bread that sustains—His very body, broken for us.

I want to live on the road *from* Emmaus to Jerusalem. I have seen
Him and I have known Him, and no matter the circumstance, I want to
run to tell the others, "It is true! All that He promised, it is true. I have
known; I have seen."

It is easy to walk that road, to believe in the better plan when I sit in
my cozy chair with my coffee in my hand and His Word opened in front
of me on my desk. But to live a life glorifying to Him, I *must* believe in
His better plan in the halls of the hospital too. I must be certain of what
I cannot yet see.

And as night falls and our van heads down the bumpy dirt road of
home, I know that I am. I am certain of His good plan for us, even when
it appears to be a terrible, ugly mess and I am certain of eternity, which
He has placed in the hearts of His people. I have known His goodness to
be true even when I can't see it yet, even if I *never* see it on this side of
eternity. I have known His goodness as the Lord who provides Himself.

I think back to the Tuesday months ago when I slipped in rainy Masese.
I came home weary, my heart and mind full. I walked through our front
doors with my head hung, ready to will myself through getting dinner
on the table and kids to bed so I could be alone with the Lord and process. But when I looked up, my breath caught in my throat as I beheld
God's faithfulness. It was a simple picture, really, one I see each day:
children piled on couches reading and gathered on the floor playing
board games, my faithful husband pouring glasses of water for dinner

and helping teenagers with homework and tickling little girls who run by. I see God's provision here and cannot deny His goodness, not even on the hardest of days.

I am an Israelite, so forgetful, and I need constant reminding. He has given us what we need—*enough*—sometimes without our even realizing it, in the routine of the day, in the ordinary and in the hard. "This is the bread that the Lord has given us to eat."[14] His perfect provision.

Later that evening, children ring the table and hold hands to pray. For nearly a decade, we've been placing our hands in one another's and bowing to the Father. Tonight we slurp spaghetti, and the big girls tell stories of "Once upon a time," recalling the names of their old baby dolls and the forts they used to build, the times they sneaked treats they weren't allowed to have and I didn't notice, and the times they got in trouble and I just about lost it. The little girls squeal with delight as they remember glimpses of it all, when they were just babies on my hip. Their daddy's eyes sparkle with love for them, and we laugh. We laugh.

I look at each of their faces. They are so grown. They have endured much in a few years of life, and they are strong and they are brave. And in all our hard and in all our joy He has been our sustenance. He has given us Himself, our daily bread, our Bread of Life.

I squeeze Benji's hand under the table as he reads us the Word. A new little life now kicks in my womb. Their first baby brother, a gift we hadn't even asked for, hadn't even known we needed. His provision, above and beyond all that we ask or imagine.

And hope is right here in this place. Beauty rises here out of the ashes, and we know in our bones that only He has brought it, only He has carried us here. He can make all things new. And He *does*.

19

BEAUTY IN
THE STORM

HE CURLS HIS TINY WHITE fist around my fingers, this sweet baby of mine who entered the world and our home a few months ago. Born right here in our home, with sisters waiting to welcome him, Noah has been our gift of peace, comfort, and joy. I memorize the curve of his fingernails, as I've done with each of my children. I feel his warm breath on my chest and breathe in the beauty of unexpected gifts. I'm not sure I ever imagined I would find myself here, yet here I am: my beloved companion at my side, beautiful young women growing up before my eyes, and this baby cradled to my chest.

Maybe I haven't gotten all the miracles I have asked for, but maybe this life, this family, is the very greatest miracle—daughters who have experienced the Lord's healing and redemption in monumental ways, who have been knit into my heart just as if they had grown in my womb, the father God knew He would give them so long before I did and the friend that He knew He would give me even during the years when I cried out in loneliness, and a son who fits right into this crazy crew, beloved by all of us as if we have never known life without him.

I look at my place, with my people, and I name it Mount Moriah, The Lord Will Provide. The literal translation of "to provide" in those Genesis verses is "to see." Here we see God. And here He sees us. When our joy is full and the kids laugh happy, and when our legs are weary and our hearts are heavy and our questions are many, He sees us. He is good to us. The Lord sees, and He will be seen.

I met a little girl a few months ago when she, her mother, and her baby sister showed up at our gate. She was thirteen years old, gentle and beautiful. She had a tumor on her leg the size of a watermelon that hurt so much she could not walk, and cancer throughout her body that would kill her in a matter of months, with or without treatment. I sat with her in the dirt and then helped her mama carry her inside. My little Patricia, who is not actually so little anymore, made them cups of tea. We sat in this sacred space and we prayed. We just prayed.

Ten years ago, I would have probably taken these people to every hospital in the country in hopes that someone somewhere would tell us something different from "terminal cancer" and that somehow we could raise money for a life-saving treatment, because I believed that God would be glorified in only the life saving. Though I shake my head as I think back on my naive faith, I smile at the passionate and ambitious young woman I used to be. Four years ago, I was so tired that I probably would have taken one look at this family and called a friend to come help them, because just the thought of walking through more suffering and death felt like enough to break me. My faith was real but so fragile, and the questions abounded. I feel great hurt for the young woman I was and unbelievable gratitude to the God who held my fragile heart and did not let go.

He saw me. He sees us.

On this day, instead of wrestling or wailing, we drank tea. We prayed. We sang worship. I asked God how we should enter into this situation and how I should share the Gospel with these precious eternal souls in front of me. As I sought His heart, I realized that I trust Him more fully than I ever really knew was possible. I prayed for the healing of this little girl and fully believed that He might choose to heal her; simultaneously, I trusted that if He did not, He would work that for His good and His glory, for the good of this mother in front of me and her baby sister and all who knew her and would touch her story. Weeks later, we visited their home and prayed. We gathered our Ugandan brothers and sisters to pray with her too. This is what it means to lay our dreams on the altar and name this place The Lord Will Provide, to fully trust that He will provide the best, the ram in the thicket.

I desire to enter fully into the joy He places before us and I desire to enter wholly into the suffering He places before us because both can be His gifts to us. Both can be made beautiful. This is our daily bread. I look back at our life and I know this now with certainty: I wouldn't trade one second of what we've been given. All the joy and all the pain right up next to each other has made a life of seeking God and knowing Him and then knowing Him more. He has shown Himself to us here.

All our stories and the intricate way they have been woven together whisper of His glory, His wild pursuit of each of us. His unending grace and love and kindness reach to us, saving us, drawing us to Him. We can be mended only if we have been broken, and so often it is in the mending that we feel most clearly His tender heart toward us. Every detail of each story is His grace, His gift to remake us in His image and rename us: His.

Not long after we prayed over her, that beautiful thirteen-year-old girl died. But she died knowing Jesus. In His beautiful and perfect timing, He brought us into her life with just enough time to share and explain His great love for her. I don't know why she had to suffer such immense pain at the end of her life. I don't know why her mother had to experience the agony of burying her daughter. But I trust that God knows even when we cannot yet see. And that is enough.

A few weeks ago, our family went out to dinner at one of our favorite little restaurants that sits on the edge of Lake Victoria. A storm was brewing behind us as we all watched the sun set over the lake. Golds, deep purples, and navy blues filled the sky and reflected off the water. It was truly beautiful.

I glanced behind me, and my breath caught in my throat. While we had all been mesmerized by the setting sun, a rainbow filled the sky behind us, right in front of the looming black clouds that were slowly rolling in. The magnitude of its beauty far surpassed that of even the sunset, but we had to be facing the storm to see it.

I tried to draw the girls' attention to the rainbow. They glanced back, but they were captivated by the sunset and searching for fish in the water and distracted by the restaurant's music and other things. Leaving the girls and their daddy studying the river, I quietly slipped off by myself, with Noah sleeping in his sling on my chest, and turned toward the black clouds to soak in the beauty of the rainbow. I thought of rainbows that God had shown us over the years, always seeming to be strategically placed at times when I needed so desperately to remember His promises and how privileged I was to partake in His beauty. It struck me, though, that if I wouldn't have turned to look into the darkness of the coming storm, I would have missed the beauty of the rainbow entirely.

So it is with life.

Would Abraham have known the beauty of the ram in the thicket if he hadn't climbed Mount Moriah with the intent of sacrificing his own son? Would Jacob have seen the face of God, known His touch, if he hadn't wrestled? Would the woman with the issue of blood have known the tenderness of His gaze or the love in His voice if she hadn't been sick, hadn't been reaching?

As I looked at the rainbow, God whispered to me a deep truth. There is much beauty to be found in a wound that is healed, in an unlikely friendship that is forged. There is much beauty to be found when the one we have nursed for hours and prayed over for many more is healed and restored, or when the child we have faithfully advised and prayed for turns back to the Truth, or any other happy ending. But there is also beauty to be found in sitting and praying by the bedside of an ill friend and holding her hand just before she slips away and looks into the face of Jesus. There is beauty to be found in the desperate and many-times-repeated unanswered prayers that have time and again ushered us to His feet. There is beauty to be found in a life poured out in faithfulness and obedience, no matter the circumstance. There is beauty to be found in the unlikely places, but in so many cases, we must be facing the storm to see it. Often, to behold this beauty, to be reminded of God's promises in such a tangible way, we must turn toward, not away from, the darkness.

The reality of living in a fallen, broken world is that there is always a storm. Headlines scream of refugees capsizing in boats as they try to flee to freedom and of women who have to choose which child gets to come with them to safety. Just twelve hours north of my home, children huddle under beds to avoid bombs. Even if they manage to survive, they face famine. About the same distance to the west of us, people gather at the site of rebel massacres to sort through piles of bodies, hoping that their loved ones are not there. The world is full of deep suffering that I know nothing of, troubles far beyond my own experience.

You also are likely facing a storm. The divorce you never wanted, the child who walks away from the path on which you tried to lead him, the family member who no longer wants relationship. You have a friend who fears a future of chemo appointments or mental hospitals or insurmountable debt, and the list goes on. It would be tempting to just close our eyes, wouldn't it?

But there is beauty to behold in the midst of the pain. I believe it. I have seen it. We must steady ourselves against the storms, friend. The temptation may be to look away, but in doing so we might miss the glory, all the beautiful ways He is remaking us through the hard.

Sometimes the things we would never pick for our lives give us opportunities to receive God's provision, to see Him working in ways we otherwise might not experience. Sometimes we are allowed to climb the mountain so that we can behold the ram in the thicket, so that we can know God all the more. It's amazing, really, that we can get exactly what we need by walking through what we never wanted. In the dry places, when our lives are not going at all as we intended, He can draw us to Him the way He always intended.

God is like that. He uses the hard things to reveal more clearly His great kindness toward us. He always knows what we need before we can even fathom it. Abraham climbs up Mount Moriah with no idea of what God could possibly be orchestrating, why God would ask him to sacrifice his only son, but God uses his faithfulness and obedience to grow his trust and prepare him for future trials. Maybe the hardest things make us the best kind of brave and the best kind of ready for all that God has next. They teach us to lean into Him time and time again because we see that it is true: *When we are weak, He is strong.*

I hadn't known this, in the beginning. I hadn't known it when I drove those long hours to visit Jane and her mom, when I welcomed them into our guest room. I hadn't known it when I cried tears over the brokenness of all the people under our roof, the pasts that seemed cruel and insurmountable, the wounds that felt like bottomless holes that wouldn't heal. I hadn't known it when I wrapped Katherine's body in a cloth to lay in her casket, when I sat alone with my tears and my Father on that bathroom floor for nights on end. I was just starting to learn it as I sat by Betty's bedside in the middle of the night, hoping for her life and preparing for her death; when we continued opening our home to others regardless of the outcome; and when I sat with our friend in the rehab unit. But now I know that the things I never wanted were the very things I needed most. The things that I thought would break me were the things that drove me straight to Him. My anguish and sorrow sent me to the Healer, who would mend all those broken places and put me back together more beautifully than I had imagined. All those cracks and holes and ruptures would be the places in my life where His glory would shine through. Beauty, though not as I expected it, would be found amid the ashes. These would be the places that taught me His heart as He lovingly and tenderly bound them up, and they would make me brave, ready for the next thing. *Ready for anything.*

We don't always remember to turn our gazes in the right direction, so we miss it, but all our mountains, all our trials, can point us toward His kindness and provision. In His great mercy, these trials are shaping us into who He designed us to be. Our God wields a chisel, yes, but He chisels not as one who would destroy but as an artist carefully, gently, kindly shaping us into who we were meant to be, tenderly drawing us to Him and all for His glory.

I walk into my sixteen-year-old's room one evening and notice that sticky notes line the wall above her bed. They are her prayers, her great hope offering to God. Some have been answered and some remain unanswered and some simply list her thanks: *Friends. Daily food. Soft words from a sister. His unstoppable love for me.* I grin. It has been a long time since my brightly colored notes lined the walls of our kitchen, my needed tangible reminders of His goodness to us.

Another day I stand barefoot under the blazing sun in the backyard and scatter sunflower seeds with Sumini, Sarah, Mary, and Patricia. Joyce walks by with her giggling baby brother on her hip. I stand surprised by joy, a joy that far exceeds circumstantial happiness, surprised by His extravagant provision, this gift, this life.

I rejoice yet again in realizing that God, who did not spare His own Son, provides the things we didn't know we needed in the first place. He knows just what we need.

The sun warms my shoulders, and I turn and look up at the house. Benji is fixing a hole in the garden fence. Ellie, Margaret, and Agnes hang laundry on the line, and Hellen, Tibita, and Scovia play Scrabble on the porch. Prossy helps Grace put on her shoes to come join us. Mack has been staying with us while he is in a time of transition, and I smile as I watch him faithfully feed our pet rabbit and hang a rope swing in the trees for our girls. Surely these days are sacred. And in this moment, the magnitude of this miracle that is our family, our life, is not lost on me. God has given grace upon grace upon grace, so much more than we deserve, so much more than I could have ever imagined. Jesus, the promised Lamb, has saved us. God has saved us! And beyond that, God has graciously, lavishly given all things we need.

It's one thing to name a place The Lord Will Provide and to believe it when the sun beats warm and life goes as planned. But it takes something sturdier, a courage only He can give, to believe it too when the night is long and the suffering is deep, when we can't yet see a ram in the thicket. It is a brave thing to hope, to continue in hope, knowing that God might say yes but that He could say no, and choosing to praise Him anyway.

And when we hope, even when hope doesn't make any sense? When we head up Mount Moriah, trembling, with the knife and the fire, the burden of the wood on our backs and no idea what is about to happen or *how* God will come through, and we say with certainty, "God will provide the lamb"? Well, then our hope puts us right up next to our loving Father. Our hope is our offering to Him, our sacrifice. And in our hope, He is shaping us, molding us, drawing us to Him. We will know Him here, friend.

Maybe today your story feels dark. Maybe the suffering and the sorrow have nearly drowned you, and the darkness threatens to swallow you up and sometimes the hurt is too much. Maybe nothing looks like a gift and nothing looks like grace. I've been there too. Maybe today life feels grand and things are going as planned but you know the bumps are up ahead because none of us get out of this life without facing a storm of some sort or another.

Now I know, and I testify: I have wrestled with God and have seen His face and felt His touch, and you will too, dear one. You will too. The God of all mercy and compassion is using our heartache to draw us to Himself and transform us into His likeness. He will turn our sorrows into joy and use our suffering to display gifts of grace. He will turn our darkness to light, and He will carry us home. *Chin up, love,* He whispers. *Hold on to that hope. Eyes on Me, dear one. I am not done yet.*

We hold on to our hope. There is always a ram in the thicket, because there is always the Lamb on the throne.

Afterword

After investing months of my life in writing and shaping this book, listening to God and pouring out my heart here, I have had the joy of reading it aloud to my family, who walked almost all of it with me. I wanted to be sure my words would honor them and their remembrances of these stories as well. The girls listened intently and smiled broadly when they heard their own names, giggling at certain details and crying with me as we each felt the sting of the losses shared here. Many contributed details from their own memories of these times and helpful thoughts to improve the storytelling.

My daughters are of such great encouragement to me. Each of them, in her own unique way, shows me kindness that I often do not deserve. They have been patient and gracious throughout the writing of this manuscript, and it has been a delight to relive these stories together and be reminded of all God has done in our lives.

As we were reading the book together, Joyce asked me if my editor might allow her to write an afterword for the book. Although I blush at the overly generous praise she has used here, I am so blessed by her heart to want to honor me in this way and share her precious words.

Katie Majors is my mother. No mother is as brilliant, gorgeous, talented, and fabulous as my sweet, awesome mother.

I know it is hard to believe, but my mother is as strong and as brave as a lion. She has been through a lot of things, but surprisingly, she still smiles. My mother is the type of woman who stands by people in every situation, no matter how hard. She is joyful and encouraging, and she listens to what you have to say. My mom is quick to pray and quick to listen to God. Then she is quick to obey what God has to say.

My mom teaches me a lot. I see God at work in her in ways that I hope He will also work in me. In places where I would be quick to say, *Really, Lord? Is this what You want?* my mother has taught me to trust Him, and I am hoping she teaches me more and more.

My mom's heart is generous, always reaching out and touching others' hearts, meeting their needs, caring for them, and listening. She speaks her heart joyfully, hoping that it can teach you and touch your heart so that you can be encouraged.

And my mom is the *best cook.*

Nothing in my life compares to my mother's love. She is a strong and encouraging person, a person who teaches me to trust in God. I am really proud to have such a wonderful mother in my life, always there for me even when I make mistakes, always ready to forgive me and help me and say, "It is okay."

I pray for my mom each day, that God would continue to bless her life and use her to do incredible things.

I love my mother because she brings glory to God not only through her gifts but also by calling out gifts and talents in others, including me. She speaks to us that we, too, can be used by God, and He works through her to shine His light into the hearts of many.

I admire my mother, and I pray that I, too, can live a life like hers, serving others first before myself. No matter what my mother goes through, she will tell you that it is okay because God has always been with her. She teaches me that I can trust Him to be with me too.

—Joyce Liberty Majors, age fourteen

REFLECTION AND
DISCUSSION GUIDE

Chapter 1: An Invitation to Hope

1. Katie writes that when she first moved to Uganda, she was "full of something that I thought was hope but in reality was more like naive optimism" (p. 4). What is the difference between optimism and hope?

2. In what ways is our view of hope sometimes distorted by cultural expectations? How might a biblical view of hope look different?

3. Read Psalm 34:17–18. The psalmist reminds us that God is near to the brokenhearted. Describe a time you experienced God's closeness in the midst of pain.

4. In what area of your life do you particularly need to know God is near you right now? What verse or phrase in Psalm 145:8–21 best helps you hold on to hope in that area?

Chapter 2: The God Wrestler

1. Why do wrestling and blessing often go together? When have you seen this proven true?

2. Read Genesis 32:24–31. Describe a time you wrestled with God, begging Him for a blessing. How did the wrestling change you? In what ways did God pursue you during that time?

3. Do you believe that God really is good, despite the brokenness you see in our world? Explain your answer.

4. What are some of the ways you have recognized God's presence even in the midst of your messiest days?

Chapter 3: In the Thicket

1. Read Genesis 12:1–3. What did God tell Abraham about where he was going? What did God promise? What did He not promise?

2. Read Genesis 22:1–18. How does God's call to Abraham in this passage initially seem to contradict God's earlier call on Abraham's life? Do you believe Abraham took Isaac to the mountain in faith or doubt? Explain your answer.

3. God's provision of a ram in the thicket for Abraham foreshadowed His giving of His Son for us. Katie writes that, because of Jesus, "all our unexpected places are also named The Lord Will Provide" (pp. 26–27). How does God's provision of the Lamb bring you hope in life's unexpectedly hard places?

4. Katie writes, "Sometimes the blessing is in the wrestling, because though we are wounded, we ache to see the face of God" (p. 23). What blessings has God given you that others might not recognize as blessings?

Chapter 4: Wounded

1. What is the difference between knowing God is good and knowing God "is good to me" (p. 31)? If you were talking with a friend who struggled to see God's goodness, what evidence could you offer to explain your belief in God's personal care?

2. Read 1 Kings 17:8–16. The prophet tells the starving widow to give her last bit of flour and oil. Right now you may feel depleted of money, time, energy, or some other resource. In what practical ways can you be faithful with what little you have?

3. Take some time to name—either aloud or on paper—some of the things you know to be true of your Savior. How does revisiting those truths affect your perspective?

4. Katie sometimes asks to see Mack's scar. Mack chuckles and says, "See what God did?" (p. 40). How do scars help us remember God's presence with us? What healing in your life can you look back on and say, "See what God did"?

Chapter 5: Prisoners of Hope

1. Read Zechariah 9:9–12. What does it mean to be a prisoner of hope?

2. Describe a time you were ashamed of your weakness. Do you believe that God is ever ashamed of you? Explain your answer.

3. Katie writes about desiring "the weak and desperate place" because it compelled her to pray "not as a discipline but as a *lifeline*" (pp. 50–51). In what ways have you experienced your weaknesses drawing you to God? Compare and contrast your prayer life in times of sorrow versus seasons of joy. What differences or similarities do you notice?

4. In contrast to a common misinterpretation of 1 Corinthians 10:13, God does often give us more than we feel we can handle. Describe a time something more than you thought you could handle proved to be a blessing in disguise.

Chapter 6: We Have One Another

1. Consider the quote from Henri Nouwen on page 55. How does this definition of compassion differ from what we commonly describe as compassion? What does it mean to build "a home" where "suffering is most acute"? Describe how Jesus did this. Consider how you could do this in your own life. Who in your world is suffering and could use true compassion, perhaps someone to sit with them?

2. Read 1 Thessalonians 2:1–12. What connections does Paul make between sharing the gospel and sharing one's life?

3. Katie writes about "the art of being interrupted" (p. 59). Why is being interrupted often uncomfortable? What reminders can we draw on to shift our perspective in those moments? What would it look like for you to practice the art of being interrupted this week?

4. From Scripture, list some examples of God using interruptions to draw people closer to Himself.

Chapter 7: A Dry and Weary Land

1. Read Psalm 63. When have you experienced extreme physical thirst? When have you been thirsty in a spiritual sense? Describe how it feels to have your physical or spiritual thirst quenched.

2. How is our faith challenged by a season of waiting? How is it strengthened in those seasons?

3. Katie writes, "Dreams die and seasons end and terrible, unspeakable things happen that don't make much sense, but God is not done with us yet. He uses the bending and the breaking and the dying to prepare the harvest, to prepare more for us" (p. 71). In what ways does hope prepare us for what God wants to do in our lives?

4. Where can we look for beauty when it seems we're waiting in the dark?

Chapter 8: Yet I Will Rejoice

1. Read Habakkuk 1:1–5. Where do you see echoes of hope in Habakkuk's desperate plea for God to show up in verses 2–4?

2. Can unanswered prayers glorify God? Why or why not?

3. What was God's response to Habakkuk in verse 5? Do you think this answer quieted his concerns? Why or why not?

4. Write your own cry to God (similar to the first verses of Habakkuk) about a situation in which you desperately long for God to

intervene. Then read Habakkuk 3:17–19 and write a similar response reflecting hope, even if you don't feel or see that hope right now.

Chapter 9: Scars

1. Read Isaiah 55:6–13. What is immediate about the imagery in this passage? What reflects a more gradual change?
2. Consider the promises God makes in verses 12–13. In view of your current circumstances and those of the people you love, does this scenario seem possible? Why or why not?
3. How does it look, practically speaking, to live out the belief that The Lord Will Provide?
4. Katie writes, "May we carry our scars not as burdens but as constant reminders of His faithfulness and goodness to us" (p. 94). Are you able to think of your relational, emotional, and physical scars not as burdens but as reminders of God's faithfulness? If so, how did you get to this place? If not, what stands in the way of a shift in your viewpoint? Write out a prayer asking God to shift your perspective to view even losses and hurts as places where He was drawing you to Himself.

Chapter 10: Come to Life

1. Describe a person who has drawn you to God not for the extraordinary things they do but for the ordinary, daily ways they practice faithfulness.
2. Do you think it's harder to be faithful while doing "extraordinary" things for God or while doing more mundane tasks? Explain your answer.
3. Read Ezekiel 37:1–14. Katie draws on this passage about God bringing new life to the people of Israel to prompt us to consider

the "hopeless dry bones" of our lives. What dry bones (such as your marriage, friendships, calling, relationship with God) do you want God to speak new life into? What would that look like?

4. What is the significance of Ezekiel's response to God in verse 3? What practices or perspectives could help you maintain an attitude of expectation, one that believes God can breathe life into the dry-bone places when you're tempted to lose hope?

Chapter 11: Choosing to Believe

1. Read Mark 5:24–34. What did the woman with the issue of blood have to overcome before she could touch Jesus?

2. In what way was this woman a prisoner of hope? How did this impact her behavior?

3. Katie writes, "How do you keep believing . . . when the last time you were wrong?" (p. 108). Describe a circumstance in which you were hesitant to hope for something. Do you believe hope is ever wasted? Why or why not?

4. What are some of the ways to renew hope by sharing our lives with others?

Chapter 12: A Flickering Flame

1. In what ways can our desperate, yet-to-be-answered need point to God's blessing and favor?

2. Read John 2:1–11. In verse 3, what did Mary want? How did her response to Jesus's words in verse 5 show her hope in Jesus?

3. Where do you see yourself in this story? As Mary, asking for wine? As the servants, doing what Jesus says? As the unknowing master? Explain your answer.

4. *Daring to Hope* explores the joy of being in secret places with God. In this chapter, Katie writes, "All this hope that doesn't make sense?

It had become my holy hiding place" (p. 120). How can hope serve as a hiding place with God?

Chapter 13: Faithful

1. Why does it take courage to be hopeful?
2. Read John 11. How do you respond to Jesus's statement and question in verse 25?
3. How have you seen this statement prove true: "Our pain does not minimize His goodness to us but, in fact, allows us to experience it in a whole new way" (p. 136)?
4. Consider John 11:5–6 and reread the first full paragraph on page 138 in *Daring to Hope.* How would you put your own situation in light of this Scripture passage: "God loves me and so He allows . . ."?

Chapter 14: Time to Sing

1. Read Song of Songs 2:10–15. How does your spirit respond to these words of invitation?
2. Have you ever been hesitant to receive God's good gifts? Why or why not?
3. Katie writes that she had forgotten how to rejoice in God (p. 149). Has this ever happened to you? What does it look like to rejoice in God?
4. How do we respond to God's blessings so that they draw us closer to Him rather than distracting us from Him?

Chapter 15: He Who Promised

1. Read Hebrews 10:19–23. Why should we have hope, according to verse 23? What does this tell us about God's character?
2. Does holding to hope "unswervingly" mean not having doubt? Why or why not?

3. What is the cost of choosing to hope? What is the potential reward?

4. How can you speak life and hope this week over someone you know who is hurting?

Chapter 16: A Deep and Quiet Love

1. Read Isaiah 61:1–3. Which phrase in these verses best describes your heart's longing, and why?

2. Read Isaiah 62:1–5. How does this passage reflect God's pursuit of us?

3. What evidence do you see in your life today that God rejoices over you?

4. Has God ever fulfilled a dream that you had given up on? In what ways did He surprise you with joy?

Chapter 17: Home

1. How would you describe what "being home" means to you?

2. Read John 21:1–14. Why did Jesus invite the disciples to breakfast?

3. Why would God want us to know Him as Friend?

4. What ordinary part of life might God be inviting you to share with Him today?

Chapter 18: Bread of Life

1. Read Luke 24:13–35. How is the story of the disciples on the road to Emmaus similar to the story of Jesus having breakfast with His disciples in John 21?

2. When has hopelessness prevented you from seeing what God is doing in your life? How does hope help us see God more clearly?

3. Katie writes, "Sometimes I think I know how God *should* act, what He *should* do, but instead He wants to walk the road with me, to

point me back to Him, to reveal Himself to me" (p. 187).
Why does God want us to have hope in Him rather than
in circumstances?

4. What manna—what sign of God's care for you—will provide
enough of what you need today to trust God for tomorrow?

Chapter 19: Beauty in the Storm

1. Read Isaiah 61:1–7. How might your personal storms uniquely
equip you to "bind up the brokenhearted" and "proclaim freedom
for the captives"?

2. What gifts can we gain through suffering?

3. How has your view of hope changed through reading this book?

4. Do you wholeheartedly believe that "everlasting joy will be yours"?
Explain your answer.

ACKNOWLEDGMENTS

So many people have walked with me on the road that led to these pages. The story God has written here would not be complete without any of you. I offer my deepest gratitude to the following people.

Benji, you teach me more about what it means to love like Jesus. Thank you for daily laying down your life to love and serve our family, for leading me closer to His heart. Thank you for choosing me. I love you.

Shana, together we have lowered too many bodies into caskets, walked too many unspeakable scenarios. But in the midst of it, we have laughed too loud and known deep joy. Your example of faithfulness ministers to our family daily. Thank you will never be enough.

Lillian and Namele, the way you love Jesus in the midst of pain and hardship is so beautiful. You challenge me to know Him more deeply, to love Him more passionately. Your lives poured out to Him are remarkable testimonies.

David, Esther, Winnie, Dan, Jamo, Princess, Musoke, Anna, Jjaja, and Simon, your stories have changed my heart toward Him in ways you might never know. Thank you for allowing me to walk them with you. It is my great honor.

The women of Masese, the children of Amazima, and the incredible Amazima staff, so many of you are behind the scenes in these stories, loving, serving, and pointing my heart toward God. I am grateful.

There are so many others. As I make a mental list of the friends who have loved us well through these pages, my heart overflows. You brought meals and stayed with the kids and helped with rides and held up my arms. You took care of us so that we could take care of others. You wrote notes of encouragement and brought brownies and sat on the kitchen floor or on hospital benches late into the night. You sent texts and e-mails with Scripture and love that spanned the ocean. You prayed. This is the body of Christ. No words suffice.

Curtis and Karen, I am so blessed by your friendship. Thank you for believing in me and for your tireless encouragement.

Laura and the rest of the team at Multnomah, thank you for believing in this story, believing that it could point people to Jesus, and for the tireless work you have put in to that end. Thank you for your commitment to pray with me and for me through the process.

Mom, Dad, and Brad. You love us well. You cheer us on. We love you.

Prossy, Margaret, Agnes, Ellie, Hellen, Mary, Tibita, Sarah, Scovia, Joyce, Sumini, Grace, Patricia, and Noah. You are my joy, my very greatest gifts. I love you.

NOTES

Chapter 1: An Invitation to Hope

1. Acts 2:46–47.

Chapter 2: The God Wrestler

1. Genesis 32:24–31.

2. See Genesis 32:26.

Chapter 3: In the Thicket

1. Genesis 12:1.

2. Genesis 12:2.

3. Genesis 15:1.

4. See Genesis 15:6.

5. Luke 1:45, NIV 2011.

6. Psalm 6:3.

7. Genesis 22:1–3.

8. Genesis 22:7–8.

9. Genesis 22:13–14.

10. See Genesis 22:8.

Chapter 4: Wounded

1. 1 Kings 17:12.

2. 1 Kings 17:13–14.

Chapter 5: Prisoners of Hope

1. Proverbs 27:7.

2. Zechariah 9:12.

3. Zechariah 2:10–11.

4. Zechariah 3:2.

5. Zechariah 3:8.

6. See Isaiah 11:1.

7. Isaiah 61:3.

8. Isaiah 61:3.

9. See Zechariah 3:4 and Revelation 19:7.

10. 2 Corinthians 1:19–22; 3:12.

11. See Isaiah 61:1–3.

Chapter 6: We Have One Another

1. Henri J. M. Nouwen, Donald P. McNeill, and Douglas A. Morrison, *Compassion: A Reflection on the Christian Life,* rev. ed. (New York: Doubleday, 2006), 25.

2. Dietrich Bonhoeffer, *Life Together: Prayerbook of the Bible,* Dietrich Bonhoeffer Works, vol. 5, trans. Daniel W. Bloesch and James H. Burtness (Minneapolis, MN: Augsburg Fortress, 1996), 34.

3. 1 Thessalonians 2:8.

Chapter 7: A Dry and Weary Land

1. See Luke 5:17–19.

2. Psalm 63:1.

Chapter 8: Yet I Will Rejoice

1. See Habakkuk 1:2.

2. Habakkuk 1:5.

3. Habakkuk 2:1.

4. Habakkuk 3:17–19.

Chapter 9: Scars

1. Isaiah 55:1.
2. Isaiah 55:1–3.
3. Isaiah 55:12–13.
4. Psalm 63:1.
5. Romans 5:2, 5.
6. Walter Wangerin Jr., *Reliving the Passion: Meditations on the Suffering, Death, and Resurrection of Jesus as Recorded in Mark* (Grand Rapids, MI: Zondervan, 1992), 31.

Chapter 10: Come to Life

1. Zack Eswine, *Sensing Jesus: Life and Ministry as a Human Being* (Wheaton, IL: Crossway, 2013), 36.
2. Ezekiel 37:1–6.
3. Ezekiel 37:13–14.

Chapter 11: Choosing to Believe

1. Mark 5:24–34.
2. Isaiah 6:1, 3.

Chapter 12: A Flickering Flame

1. Isaiah 45:3.
2. See Luke 22:43.
3. Psalm 63:1.
4. Psalm 63:2–4.
5. Psalm 63:5–8.
6. Hillsong Live, "Healer," by Michael Guglielmucci, *This Is Our God,* copyright © 2008, Hillsong.

7. Revelation 21:1–2.

8. Revelation 21:3–7, NIV 2011.

9. Revelation 21:22–23.

10. Revelation 22:1–5.

11. Revelation 22:20.

Chapter 13: Faithful

1. John 11:32.

2. John 11:25–26.

3. John 11:5–6, NIV 2011.

4. John 11:36.

Chapter 14: Time to Sing

1. Isaiah 61:3.

2. Song of Songs 2:10–13, NIV 2011.

3. Song of Songs 2:14.

4. Song of Songs 2:10, 14–15.

Chapter 15: He Who Promised

1. Hebrews 10:23.

2. Hebrews 10:23.

Chapter 16: A Deep and Quiet Love

1. Isaiah 61:3.

2. Isaiah 62:2–5, NIV 2011.

Chapter 17: Home

1. See Matthew 4:19.

2. See John 21:6–7.

3. John 21:12.

4. 1 Corinthians 2:9.

Chapter 18: Bread of Life

1. Sandra McCracken, "In Feast or Fallow," *In Feast or Fallow,* copyright © 2010, Drink Your Tea Music (ASCAP), admin. by Simpleville Music Inc.

2. See Exodus 14:12.

3. Exodus 16:4.

4. Exodus 16:15.

5. 1 Peter 2:3.

6. Luke 24:15–16.

7. Luke 24:21.

8. Luke 24:26–27, NIV 2011.

9. Luke 24:28–35, NIV 2011.

10. Luke 24:30–31.

11. See Matthew 26:26.

12. Luke 24:33.

13. See John 20:25.

14. See John 6:58.

A M A Z I M A

M I N I S T R I E S

Founded by Katie Davis Majors in 2008 and fueled by the conviction that God cares for the poor and vulnerable, Amazima Ministries is on a mission to educate and empower women, children, and families in Uganda. Amazima's financial partners make it possible for the gospel to be proclaimed every day as hundreds experience the hope of Jesus in tangible ways.

JOIN AMAZIMA IN BRINGING **HOPE**
TO THE PEOPLE OF UGANDA.
amazima.org/hope